Issues of the Heart

ISSUES *of the* HEART

PERSONAL STORIES OF FAITH TO ENCOURAGE AND CHALLENGE YOU

SAMUEL R. SILIGATO III

XULON PRESS

Xulon Press
2301 Lucien Way #415
Maitland, FL 32751
407.339.4217
www.xulonpress.com

Unless otherwise indicated, Scripture quotations taken from the King James
Version (KJV) – *public domain.*

Cover Photo: Sunset at Fortescue, NJ- taken by Sam Siligato.

Paperback ISBN-13: 978-1-66286-274-8
Ebook ISBN-13: 978-1-66286-275-5

DEDICATION

As this book came together it became evident as to whom it should be dedicated. Grace Benfer-Bostwick is not my birth mother, but she and her husband Harry were there for my spiritual birth and I consider them my spiritual parents. These past fifty years she has invested in my life in many ways. To say she is special is an understatement. The Lord used Grace to give me insights for several of these stories. Multitudes have been blessed because their lives have crossed paths with hers. She is a godly woman who has given a life of service to the Lord, and one of the sweetest, kindest souls a person could ever meet.

I am honored to know Grace and to be a part of her life, and I am blessed to have her in my life.

Amazing Grace
Twas Grace that taught my heart to fear,
(She and husband Harry
when I first started my walk with the Lord at age sixteen)
And Grace my fears relieved,
(through her counsel and prayers over the course of a half century)

ACKNOWLEDGMENTS

My wife Sherry invested countless hours of help editing my rough drafts. She made good use of her red pens while helping these stories to their final form. As a spouse of a writer, she sacrificed many hours of family time as I pursued completion of this book.

Dr. MaryAnn Diorio lit the fire in me to become a writer many years ago. As an initial writing mentor her instruction was instrumental in helping me overcome the fear of just starting out as a writer. She is a good friend, and her advice as this book neared completion was invaluable and appreciated.

I want to shout out to my friend Trish, who is my sister from a different set of parents. She dragged me across the finish line to completion of this book. She spent hours editing, formatting, helping with the cover, and much general preparation of the manuscript to its electronic form. Trish offered the encouraging, but sometimes "pushy" support only a sister could get away with. Without her help I might still be looking at a collection of papers and manila folders.

Thank you Jeanie, for your help with the pictures, and to Sharon for your editing investment.

I am grateful to all who were gracious enough to read the manuscript before publication and offer their opinions and suggestions. Thank you, Christy, Susan, Carol, Dan, Sharon, David, and Jason.

I have always been appreciative to the Lord for giving me the desire to write, and not giving up on me over the many delays. I hope to honor Him with my words, and be faithful to the calling He has given.

CORNERSTONE:

An organization dear to my heart

E ach and every one of us is special in God's sight. We may even be His Crowning Achievement! I bet we are! God tells the prophet Jeremiah that He has thoughts for us for peace and to give us a future and a hope. Jeremiah chapter twenty nine says that He knew us before the womb, and before we were born He sanctified us.

Psalm 139 says that He (God) formed our parts and covered us in our mother's womb. We are fearfully and wonderfully made, and we were not hidden from Him when we were made in secret. The gift of life is our most precious gift!

I am privileged to share a portion of the proceeds from the sale of each book with Cornerstone Women's Resource Center in Salem, New Jersey.

Cornerstone is a faith based, pro-life, donor supported, non-profit organization that has been providing no-cost, life-affirming support in Salem and Cumberland Counties, NJ, since 1983. They provide free pregnancy testing, ultrasounds, and options information to abortion-minded women in order to help them choose life for their babies. Additional services include the Earn As You Learn parenting program, Pregnancy Loss Recovery, and the Get Real Healthy Relationship program for middle/high school students. Cornerstone's vision is to be the #1 preferred choice for those facing an unplanned pregnancy. For more information, please call 856-935-0304, email at info@cornerstonewrc.org or visit their supporter website at PathtoLifePartners.org.

Psalm 22:10 "From my mother's womb you have been my God."

WITH GRATITUDE

I am thankful for my parents Sam and Louise who gave me life and have been a support for me ever since. Their seventy years of marriage is a testament to commitment.

My wife Sherry was a life saver as I explain in one of my stories in this book. You have given me the best years of my life! Your love has been unconditional and a strength for me.

My daughters Jean, Faith, and Samantha; and sons-in-law Jason, Tim, and Jeff; grandchildren, Timmy, Ashton, Jackson, Josanna, Ethan, Julia, and Evangeline have been a constant blessing in my life.

I am fortunate to have many good and faithful friends, several of which I have known over fifty years. You all have given a lifetime of friendship and influence. I am very grateful for you.

My own sister Karen passed away in 2001 at the age of forty-four. I miss her but know I will see her again. My friend Trish, whom I call Sister, has filled much of the sister void in my life. Sis, you have been a blessing to me and my wife and our family.

Pastor Gerritt Kenyon was my first pastor for several years as I began my walk with the Lord. He and his entire family are some of the most committed individuals I have ever known. I will always remember one of his sayings that has served me well in life; "If we do our best, God will do the rest!"

Pastor Woodson Moore was my pastor for nearly forty years before he went on to Glory. He left a huge imprint on me and my family. Pastor would always say "You're not living if you're not giving."

The baton was passed to my current pastor, Ken Corson. He and his wife Tiffany are leading us as the Lord directs in the years ahead. Pastor likes to say "let your mess become your message, and let your test become your testimony!"

To all of you – thank you for being in my life.

Table of Contents

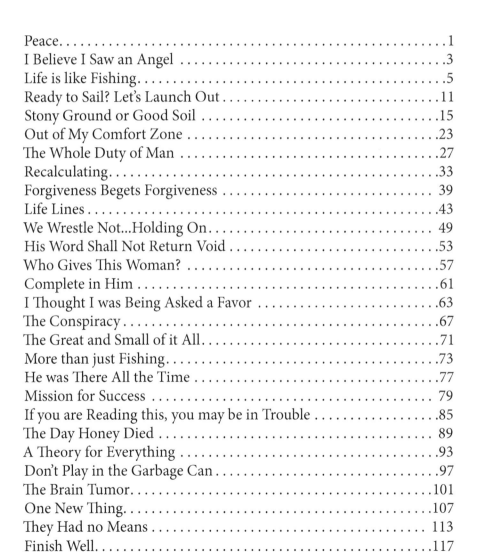

FOREWORD

I have known the author of *Issues Of The Heart*, Sam Siligato, for a long time. You will read about his athletic ability and how he rarely let a ball get through while he was playing shortstop for the church softball team. What he does not mention was the outstanding and modest third baseman that would range to his left to plug the left side hole on more than one occasion. That would be me! Get ready for more smiles and tears!

Having read the manuscript in preparing for the writing of this Foreword, I discovered a unique ability by Sam to articulate and link transparently his life's experiences with the truths found in the Word of God.

I can assure you that as you read this book, you will find yourself identifying with different circumstances in your own life, likened to those which Sam wrestled with starting with the moment he gave his heart to the Lord at the age of sixteen.

Sam encourages and exhorts the reader to never give up no matter what you are facing. Note: I personally experienced that encouragement and exhortation as I read the manuscript during the exact time my wife and I were facing the challenge of caring for her mother in our home when she could no longer care for herself. Was that a "coincidence"? Or, was it God's way of giving us just what we needed when we needed it?

Issues Of The Heart, is a compilation of God's refreshing, peaceful, loving and purposeful ways of overwhelming us with His "springs and fountains" flowing from His throne room, causing life and light where and when death and darkness try to overtake us.

As a Christian Counselor for nearly forty years, I have seen repeatedly, people looking for answers to the circumstances they face. I have always told my students and those I have counseled, that if you want to know the answer to what you should do, visualize yourself walking to the foot of the cross with Jesus hanging there in agony, as He lays down His life for your eternal salvation, and look up! Jesus is the answer to all our questions.

What you will find as you read through the pages of this book, are the keys to the spiritual connection that God offers to all of us who need to strengthen our relationship with Him through His Son Jesus Christ.

Sam takes you on a journey of testimonies from his life that gave him the grace to be an overcomer and experience victory in the face of fierce adversity.

You will find the heart of a man whose life has been changed and directed by God. Sam has given us the example of what humility, loyalty, compassion, and a good sense of humor will do when you need a good dose of joy to get you through.

Sam has been blessed with his sweet, beautiful, and talented wife, Sherry. From their marriage they have produced three lovely and godly daughters, Jeanie, Faith and Samantha. One of my fondest memories was visiting them one Christmas when they were little girls and Barbara and I giving them each a doll. As of this writing they all have their own babies, seven in all.

The King James version of the Bible says in Proverbs 4:23, "Keep your heart with all diligence for from it are the issues of life." Other versions have "guard" for "keep", and "springs and fountains" for "issues". (Go to the Hebrew in Strong's Concordance 2416 for the original translation of "issues"!)

As you read this book, I trust your life will be refreshed as Sam Siligato diligently and with excellence, pours into your life, encouragement and exhortation to do your very best to find God's will for your life and purpose in your heart to always bring Him glory.

Rev. Dr. Harold Hart, Jr. is the Pastor of Counseling at Life Church in Williamstown, NJ (10 years) and served as Pastor of Counseling and Men's Ministries at Fairton Christian Center, Fairton, New Jersey (28 years). Since his retirement from *secular employment in July 2013, he has had a private Christian Counseling ministry at his home office. He is a Professional Member of the American Association of Christian Counselors, Licensed with the Assembly of God in New Jersey in 1988 and with the Fellowship Network in Texas in 1995, and a Professor at the Southern Campus at the New Jersey School of Ministry of the Assemblies of God. He is an author, teacher, and speaker. He lives in Millville, New Jersey with his wife Barbara.

*For most of his secular employment, Dr. Hart was the Corporate Environmental, Health, and Safety Regulatory Compliance Director for several large corporations in the Americas (Continental USA, Puerto Rico, and Canada to South America) and Globally in a number of European countries.

Introduction

Sometimes things in life take a long time to come to fruition. This book is one of those things. Many years in the works, there were delays and even periods when this project lay on the back burner. Life can do that at times. By the grace of God and help of others we finally crossed the finish line.

My hope is that *Issues of the Heart* will be a blessing and encouragement, and that readers will enjoy the essays, identify with some, and gain individual insights and perspectives. Additionally, my desire for these pages is they would find their way to individuals who may be still searching for the Truth. That these stories, in turn, would help in coming to an understanding of the love of God and His benefits and blessings.

As an article or book is published, its influence can be far reaching especially with the social media platforms today. When I teach and write, I like to use analogies. I could imagine a quiver full of arrows being shot into the air in all directions not knowing where they land. Our words are like those arrows. They can reach individuals throughout the world, hopefully with a positive impact. I pray these arrows (words) achieve the destination the Lord would have for them.

Please see the feedback page at the end of the book. We would love to hear from you and learn where some of the arrows have landed! Be Blessed!

Peace

Have you ever needed to get away to a quiet place to clear your head, find some direction, or just enjoy some time in the outdoors—by yourself—in a desperate search for some peace? In 2 Thessalonians 3:16 we read, "Now the Lord of peace himself give you peace always by all means." There have been many times that I needed just that.

One time in particular, I traveled a short distance to one of my favorite places near my home. As I sat on an old wooden bridge in the middle of the marshland, I began to seek God for an answer for a particular decision that was before me.

It was a warm, breezy, early Fall morning in Southern New Jersey. The decision before me was one that could drastically affect the rest of my life. The past year brought a few such decisions, some of which were behind me now. I had been in turmoil for several days, and I sought peace about the situation.

Sitting on that bridge, I looked about. The reeds rustled in the breeze, the sky a magnificent blue—the view breathtaking! To the west lay the bay, and to the east, a tree line on the horizon. In between and all around was the beautiful marsh. I sensed God was there in the center of some of His wonderful creation.

I prayed aloud, "Lord, I need peace, please speak to me." I must admit that I have never heard an audible voice from God. However, there have been times that I have had a distinct impression or there has been some physical evidence that I have interpreted as that "still small voice of God."

As I prayed, a seagull flew by me and landed about ten yards from me in the middle of the creek which wound under the bridge. It just sat there—looking at me—peacefully.

Now, one of the things known about South Jersey and the shore areas is that we have an abundance of seagulls. Oftentimes they are aggressive, pesky nuisances, trying to grab your food and violate your space. Believe it or not, "my seagull" was the only one that I would see that day. Being still, it just looked at me—no aggression—nothing—just floating in the water.

As I asked the Lord again to speak to my heart and give me peace about my situation, I looked about, then said "Oh, I see now. You are speaking. I am just not listening!" For all about me WAS peace. In the solitude, I could sense the Lord's voice and His hand in the nature and wildlife around me. I began to have peace of mind, of soul, and in my heart. This was the peace of God.

Philippians 4:7 says, "And the peace of God which passeth all under-standing, shall keep your hearts and minds through Christ Jesus."

Each of us should have a special place where we feel closest to the Lord. For me, it is being along the beach or at a water's edge. Finding our place and getting alone with the Lord is very refreshing—and peaceful! When we do get alone with Him and ask Him to speak to us, it might be a good idea if we don't do ALL of the talking by allowing time to be spoken TO. Listen and look for His still, small voice as we allow him to speak to our hearts, and we will find the peace of God ruling in our hearts and minds.

I Believe I saw an Angel

It was five days before my younger sister Karen would pass away on September 13, 2001. My wife and I drove to the Ocean City boardwalk in New Jersey, a place we very much enjoyed because we were by the ocean and beach. Ocean City was one of my sister's favorite places as well.

Knowing full well that my sister would soon succumb to her valiant battle with cancer at the age of forty-four, my wife and I needed to be at our place of peace during this difficult time. We strolled many blocks to the north end of the boardwalk and found a bench to sit on and look out over the ocean. The constant sound of the waves as they came ashore was always comforting to me.

Behind us was a large pier full of amusement rides. The predominant ride was a very tall ferris wheel. It yielded a significant and heart-rending memory. One of my sister's last wishes was to be able to ride the wheel once more. My brother- in- law made her wish come true as he was able to transport my sister there in her last days for just one more ride.

Sunset was fast approaching, and the sky was a magnificent pink and blue, then orange and blue, and finally red. For some reason it made me feel that all would be well.

My attention was then turned toward the ocean. A rock jetty protruded far from the shoreline. On the jetty was a man fully dressed in Scottish attire. He started to play "Amazing Grace" on the bagpipes. I could not believe what I was seeing and hearing... my favorite hymn played exceptionally well with such feeling and emotion on the bagpipes!

I tried to reason where such a man came from, how did he get on the rock pile, and why would he be playing "Amazing Grace"? I was so blessed and ministered to. I came to believe that this man must have been sent by God as messenger of peace and comfort to me. You can come to your own conclusion, but I will never be convinced otherwise. As the "man" finished, he walked off the jetty and headed down the beach. I watched him intently fully expecting him to disappear, until I could see him no more. I regret to this day not jumping up from the bench to run to the beach and poke the man to see if he was real.

Hebrews 13:1 says, "Be not forgetful to entertain strangers: for thereby some have entertained angels unawares." Maybe you have seen an angel in your lifetime, and you were not aware of such. Possibly YOU have been an angel to someone at some point. Perhaps you made a call to someone at a very critical point in their life, or sent a note that was received in a moment of loneliness or depression that uplifted them, maybe in their own walk in the "valley of the shadow of death." Perhaps you could have volunteered to help in any one of many capacities, making a dinner or giving a gift or money in a very needed time.

I believe that we all have opportunities in our lives to become an "angel" to someone. We may not know the individual or realize the opportunity until we get to heaven someday—or then again, we may.

I had the opportunity to give the eulogy at my sister's funeral and shared the "angel story" with everyone. When we got to the grave-side service, it was asked of the family if there was a particular hymn we wanted to sing. One gentleman spoke up, "How about Amazing Grace"?...and so we did!

Life is like Fishing

As a real estate agent for over thirty years, many times I have said that real estate is like fishing. I would apply my fishing analogy to various aspects of the real estate transaction. Sometimes my clients would chuckle, but many times the lesson of the analogy would bring insight to the particular situation at hand.

Such is life itself. A lot like fishing. Anyone who has fished any length of time is aware of the range of feelings, situations, and outcomes that can be part of any fishing experience.

From the time we plan to go fishing until the actual day of the trip, there is anticipation of a successful day. Hopefully we experience the same feeling when we embark on a new project, journey, personal event, or vacation. It is God's desire for us to have a full and abundant life filled with days that bring us joy. (John 10:10)

In our fishing adventure, joy can be a product of a successful day, whether in number of fish caught, or the size of the fish, as even one prize fish can make our day. The experience itself can be a cause of joy because of a beautiful, peaceful day on the water, or the fellowship with friends and family.

Our abundant life can be composed of success in business and goals, relationships established with a spouse, family, or friends —the "Kodak moments" if you will. These will be memories to be held dearly throughout life.

When my friends and I plan a fishing trip we always hope to catch as many fish as possible, and sometimes that is the case. Many times though, we find ourselves saying, "Well, at least it is a great day to be on the water even if we are not catching so many." A life analogy might be even though we do not always achieve the success we set out to accomplish, there is much more to life in the people we live with, those we have an opportunity to meet and help and share with, and the legacy we make.

Anyone who has fished knows that patience is a prime ingredient to be kept in our tackle box. How many of us know we do not always catch a fish in the first cast? Or the second? I could go on of course. Sure there are times when we catch a fish immediately. I have had days when the catch was fast and steady, but those days are the exception. Most of the time it is hit or miss, maybe with a hot stretch, then a slow period. There were days when no fish were caught. A few times I only caught one fish at the end of the day. Once in a while, that last lone fish was the one that made my day!

It is not so hard to be patient in life when things are moving along, going great. During intermittent times of success and failure, victory and defeat, we might find it challenging to stay focused on our mission and purpose in life. Patience (long suffering) is one of the fruits of the Spirit. (Galatians 5:22) Patience, they say, is a virtue. One definition of virtue is an admirable quality, merit, or accomplishment.

The enemy would have us get frustrated with life and take our eyes off of the good and blessings that have been bestowed upon us. Also, should we become impatient in a current status in our life, we might be tempted to abandon our prescribed course and gaze towards areas that we might perceive as "greener grass." When things don't go well all the time, we should be reminded these phases are part of life and Jesus will see us through any trial.

On days when I caught no fish, I admit that my patience would wear thin. There were days without any bites at all, and that was more than frustrating. A possible explanation might include I was fishing in the wrong spot. If we are out of the Lord's Will for our life, things could get frustrating, and the "pickings" slim. If we realize this is the case, it is best to "move the boat", so to speak. We should make a move in our lives to get back into the Will of the Lord.

Sometimes a lack of catch is not a result of anything we did wrong. Water temperatures, atmospheric pressure, tides, or just the absence of fish are contributing factors. Spiritually speaking we can be doing all the right things—reading the Word, praying, going to church, etc, yet we lack some answers we have been seeking.

Perhaps the timing was not right for a particular day of fishing. Our fishing experience tells us to try another day. In our walk with the Lord, we are to run the race, stay the course, and rest assured that the Lord is always with us. The answers will come. The only time we lose is if we give up and not finish our course.

Many days we were drifting along having a great time. Life was good. Then all of a sudden one of us would get snagged on some unseen obstacle. If the affected fisherman could not free his line immediately, the rest of us would have to wind in our lines in order for the boat to be maneuvered in such a way to possibly free the snagged line. The boat would be positioned to the left and to the right, or go back in the opposite direction all in hopes of having the line escape its unknown captor. If this effort was not effective, the last resort was to cut the line and there would be no hope for the tangled rig.

Sometimes, as we cruise through life we too can become snagged. We could get hung up on an unforeseen problem such as loss of job, a broken relationship, unfaithfulness of a friend, or perhaps an injury. Other times we get snagged as a result of poor choices we make. We knew there were risks in our choices and were aware of the pitfalls and dangers that lurked. We saw the buoys (markers) that warned of danger, yet we tried to traverse the waters anyway. Proverbs is full of warnings that would keep us from waters containing items that lie in wait for the unsuspecting and unwise. These hazards that would like to snag us e wiles and schemes of the devil as mentioned in Ephesians ix...WATCH OUT!

the fishing boat, when we get snagged in life, often times we are not the only ones affected. Others might have to make adjustments because of our predicament. On occasion we can free the snagged line without consequences. Sometimes in life, the line will be cut with no chance of seeing a relationship restored. We would do well to avoid known hazardous areas in our lives so that we would not become entangled to the point of affecting others, or possibly causing irreparable damage to ourselves. Men, you might guess one of the areas I am talking about here.

Perseverance is akin to patience. I do not know of any fisherman that expects to catch his limit of fish in the first few minutes of the trip. We must work through the slow times and the disappointment of not attaining immediate gratification. Some in our society are of the mentality of "I want it now!" They want no parts of having to persevere through a time. In Luke 5:5, we hear the soon to be followers of Jesus say, "Master we have worked hard all night and haven't caught anything." Of course the verse does not stop here. It goes on to say "But because you say so, I will let the nets down." (NIV) The followers persevered, and because they did so they were rewarded and blessed for a lifetime.

It is normal to feel disappointed after a drought period in life. However if we persevere according to His Will, we can be assured our slow season will turn into success. We must persevere. We must keep 'letting the nets down" until we realize our goal, our victory in matters of life. If you are praying for 'that right person' to come into your life, persevere in prayer and faith and be patient for the Lord's timing. That "keeper," the catch of your life, may only be one cast away!

Once a fish is hooked it is important to keep you pole and line taut. A slack line will give the fish more of an opportunity to work itself free. Stay focused, keep the line tight...and REEL BABY! Do all that you can to get that prize fish in the boat. The Scripture says "Whatever you set your hand to do, do with all your might as unto the Lord." You can apply this scripture here if you want. Regardless, it should be applied to all areas in our life. Moral of this paragraph?...Don't be a slacker!

We've all heard the story about "the one that got away." I could tell you a few. The biggest flounder I ever caught was missed multiple times by the netter as the fish lay on top of the water, looking at us, seemingly saying "Ha ha, you missed me!" Then it took a dive to freedom! It makes for good stories sometimes but often is accompanied by feelings of sadness and regret, feelings which, if we allow them, will make us lose sight of all the good in the day.

Similarly if we allow regrets in life to rule our thinking, this will be harmful. If we are fixated on the "what if's"—-what if I had taken the other job, gone to the other school, or married the other person, we will lose sight of the blessings before us. Philippians 3:13 tells us to forget what is behind and strain toward what is ahead. Let's do it!

There are many ways to measure success. This past year while fishing in the back bays of the New Jersey shore, on a trip with two of my life-long friends, we caught a total of 125 flounder! It is the boat record for a day; however, we did not catch even one keeper with a minimum size of eighteen inches. Success or not? My wife and I went out on two occasions. One trip we caught only four fish, but three were keepers. The other trip yielded only five fish, but four of them were keepers. Success or not? Other trips saw different totals and ratios of keeper fish. Bottom line (no pun intended) each time we were doing what we wanted to do and that was to fish. Usually the weather was great and we got to spend time with each other and our friends, while making memories and having fresh flounder to feast upon. I call it "from the sea to me!" Success or not?

Life successes are also measured in various ways. Some measure by the status of jobs or education. Some by the size of bank accounts or houses. How many and how new are the cars that are owned. Please note that I do not see anything wrong with attaining the above mentioned. These things can be the product of hard work and much time invested in a skill, talent, call, or occupation. The parable of the talents is just one example how the Lord can bless.

Success is not only measured by how much or how many. If I may quote Clarence the guardian angel from the movie classic *Its a Wonderful Life*, "No man is a failure who has friends." My former Pastor, Woodson Moore said on occasion, "You are successful when you reach out to help others."

One of the sweetest sounds to a fisherman's ears is that of a prize catch flopping around in the cooler! Success at last, the catch of the day that made all of the preparations, time, and cost of the fishing trip worthwhile. The sound of the keeper in the cooler makes us want to come back for more. We cannot wait until the next trip!

Now, I do not mean ANY DISRESPECT with this analogy. The Bible tells us in Luke 15:10, that the angels in heaven rejoice when a soul comes to the knowledge and acceptance of the Lord. (NIV) There is a new name written down in glory. I believe in the natural, we fish for the prize keepers and rejoice when we achieve our goal and get to place them in the cooler. Likewise, if we are fishers of men we will rejoice when a lost soul finds the Lord. They become a "keeper" and get placed in the Kingdom. If we had a part in their "catch," so much more the rejoicing! We will have attained our star for the day. Soul winners will shine as stars. Daniel 12:3 says, "Those who are wise will shine like the brightness of the heavens, and those who lead many to righteousness, like the stars forever and ever."(NIV)

Ready to Sail?
(Let's Launch Out!)

I love being on a boat! There's something about cruising on the water that brings a peace. My wife and I enjoy fishing in the back bays of the Jersey shore, where waters are usually calm, and there is an abundance of wildlife to appreciate (and if we are really fortunate, we catch some fish too).

The Bible has several stories that take place on or near the water. One of which is found in the familiar passage of Luke 5: 4-11. Jesus told Peter to "Launch out into the deep," and let his nets down for a "draught" of fish. Even though Peter had toiled all night without catching any fish, he was still obedient to the Lord. Perhaps Peter obeyed out of love for the Master or he had faith that a miracle was about to occur.

It is important to note that Jesus launched out with Peter. I am reminded of Hebrews 13:5, where it says "I will never leave you or forsake you," and in Matthew 28:20 Jesus says "And lo, I am with you always, even to the end of the world. Amen". Of course the draught (or multitude) of fish were netted to the point of the nets being on the verge of breaking, and even the boat might have sunk. The "catch of fish" was miraculous!

Now, let's take another look at "launch out into the deep." Could this be symbolic of another message that Jesus has for us? Please allow me some latitude here (writers are allowed you know). You get to judge and determine for yourself.

Matthew Henry, a Presbyterian theologian from the seventeenth century, in his commentary states; "how deep we should launch out, He (Jesus) does not say. The depth unto which we launch will depend on how perfectly we have given up the shore and the greatness of our need and the apprehension of our possibilities. The fish were to be found in the deep, not shallow water."

Our needs are to be found in the deep things of God. We should launch out into the deep of God's Word. Psalm 42:7 says "deep calls unto deep." In Proverbs 20:5 we read that the heart of man is like deep water. Daniel 2:22 states "he revealeth the deep and secret things. He knoweth what is in the darkness."

So, how deep we should launch, we are not told. I believe that is different for each one of us. The depth will be determined by how perfectly we give up the shore. The shore could represent our comfort zone or easy place.

Just to be clear—I LOVE THE BEACH!—-the shore (we are beach people). Sometimes though, we need to step off the shoreline and into the water. Sometimes we need a boat to launch out. We need to get out of our comfort zone (ouch—yes, I feel that pain too!). What is it that the Lord wants from us? What might He be telling us to do?

The greatness of our need can also determine the depth to which we need to launch. What needs do we have that require God's intervention in our lives be they spiritual, physical, financial, or social? Can we have the faith of Peter when he launched out at Jesus' word?

Finally, the "apprehension of our possibilities." Are you called to be a pastor, an evangelist, a missionary, a teacher, a singer, a writer, or a minister of helps? We need to be willing to launch out to the depths required to attain our calling. We should be faithful and diligent in our pursuits.

Why don't we launch out sometimes? Perhaps we don't want to, or feel we are not qualified. Maybe we are afraid. Psalm 34:4 says, "I sought the Lord, and He heard me, and delivered me from all of my fears."

So, "ALL ABOARD"! Get your sailing gear ready! Jesus will be our life preserver as we are faithful to His call…and the "catch of fish" that awaits – well—I for one, believe that could be representative of the blessings God has in store for us!

JUST SAYIN'

Stony Ground or Good Soil

I will forever remember my spiritual birthday May 12, 1971. I was sixteen years old. I spent my early elementary years in a Catholic school and church and learned many of the stories as well as some general knowledge of the Bible. While in my young teens, I do not remember attending church much. It was not due to a lack of effort from my mother because she wanted me to go, but it was my rebellion against even having to go to church at all.

As a freshman in high school, parents of one of my best friends took me to an Assembly of God church in a neighboring town —an interesting experience for a Catholic boy! They also encouraged me and facilitated my attending a Christian camp for a winter week. The experience was a good one as the kids were great. We had fun, and the chapel sessions were tolerable from my perspective. The speakers were sincere and the messages were ones that young people needed to hear, but I remember just being there for the fun experience of camp and not so much for the spiritual aspect. And besides, ice cream usually followed the service!

Thanks to the influence of friends at the end of my sophomore year, I began to attend a local Assembly Church. I do not recall a spiritual drawing to the early visits to this church. My guy friends invited me to the services and youth group, but truth be told there was a young lady from school who had caught my eye and just happened to be attending the same church. What a coincidence!

As Providence would have it—yes, I know it was Providence, I began to get close to the young lady's family. After a couple of weeks, there was a city wide crusade in town. Since I was not driving yet, this wonderful family offered to pick me up and take me to the crusade each night. It was different for me for sure, but the preacher's messages started to make me think about how I viewed God, my purpose in life, and about my soul and spirit in the light of eternity. I would also hear messages about God's love for us and how we needed a relationship with God the Father, Jesus the Son, and the Holy Spirit. I knew of the Trinity, but never really thought much about my relationship with God.

By midweek, as the alter calls were given, I would start to feel uncomfortable sitting in my seat. Fifty years later I still remember that feeling. My heart would start to beat faster, and I would sweat a little. It got to the point where I thought my heart would pop out of my chest! I honestly did not know what was going on. After the second time I mentioned this to a friend; he explained it was most likely the Holy Spirit ministering to my heart. I was being "called" to accept Jesus into my life as Lord and Savior. The next time it happened I finally said, "Okay, okay, I will go forward— but wait until the last night at the youth rally." I hope the Lord chuckled at my stubbornness and attempted control of the situation!

I DID go forward at the youth rally. I still remember the preacher's name and part of the message. To this day, I am grateful to the family who invested in me and were instruments that helped change the course of my life. As it happened, I became very close with them. They treated me like a son and became my "spiritual Mom and Dad." Matthew chapter thirteen, speaks of the parable of the seeds that fall in different areas. Some fall in the sun and wither and die. Others fall among the weeds and get choked out. Some fall on stony ground and thrive for a bit, but eventually die because there is not nutrition and soil for them to take good root. Then there is the good soil where the seed gets water and nourishment and is able to thrive and bear fruit. My spiritual parents were the "garden and good soil" that helped my walk with the Lord to take root and not die quickly as was the fate of the seed that fell on stony ground.

Not only were my spiritual parents the good soil, but a sweet fragrance emanated from their "garden." I sensed then, but did not fully understand the scriptural reference of that fragrance. In Philippians chapter four, Paul speaks of the sweet savor we should exhibit, and my friends were just that! Each of us can have a profound impact on others by our words and encouragement in things of the Lord. We may be conscious of the impact, or maybe not in some instances—only to find out later in life—- or maybe in eternity.

The seeds we plant may sprout immediately or may grow in a season or two. 1 Corinthians 3:6, speaks of being planted, watered, and then the Lord will make the growth. All of these are vital and instrumental and can have an eternal effect on those with whom we come in contact. I remember hearing a statistic from the Billy Graham Association where only one third of those going forward to accept Jesus into their heart sustained a lasting relationship with the Lord. I wonder what happened to the others. My guess in many cases is that they had limited, or no good soil to fall into. How important for us to help, encourage, and even mentor in some way those "newborn" into the Kingdom.

I remember being one such newborn. I wanted to tell everyone as I proceeded to share my story. Now fifty years later I remember the feelings, but those thoughts are tempered by the realization that I may have been "too excited" and came across at times as being overbearing. I believe we can accomplish the most for the Lord by doing what He tells us to do. Love God, love our neighbors as ourselves, forgive, do unto others as we would have them do unto us, and be salt and light. We do not need to beat people over the head with our Bibles. We just need to tell them about our Lord in love, with our words and deeds.

At that time in my life I desired the "sincere milk of the Word." My heart was open and tender to the things of the Lord, and one way that manifested itself was in my early writing as a teen. Recently, I stumbled upon a folder that I had forgotten about which contained several poems that I will share in the pages to follow. It is interesting I never wrote any poems after those two years in high school. Perhaps it was just a way of expressing my feelings at the time. My hope is that they minister to you, the reader, as well. From the heart of a seventeen and eighteen year old.

One True Friend

There is one friend above all others,
One friend there is indeed.
For He and only He can do all things,
And meet your every need.

I was a boy young at heart
Problem filled night and day.
I thought I had a great life's start,
But passed along the way.

And then one day my heart was filled,
Filled like the bright of day.
My eyes, they too were opened wide,
My soul could feel the rays.

And now for Christ I try to live,
In each and every way.
One True Friend He has been,
Who leads me day by day.

His Word

His Word to me is a way of Life,
A way of life so good.
Words true, sincere and meaningful,
Words standing longer than any words could.

The inspiration of His Word
Keeps me day by day.
It shows me which way to go,
Each and every way.

His Word contains much knowledge,
Many morals too.
The Bible is the book
That should be read by you.

Though in many versions
It's got messages worth looking for.
Though some be old in age,
I'm sure you'll find an inner peace in every page.
The testaments both New and Old,
Have stories many times told.
They show you many a plan
That shows you how you may grasp Jesus's hand.

An Easter Poem

Why oh why was He crucified?
Why oh why did He die?
Why oh why did He come to earth?
Tell me why, tell me why, oh why

Born of the Virgin Mary
Conceived of the Holy Ghost
More than just ordinary,
A Savior to be for most.

As life progressed those thirty years
He showed His love and grace.
If one believed in Him alone
One was saved by hope and faith.

His last three years He did perform
Many wondrous things.
He healed the sick and cured the blind
Rose the dead and changed the wine.

The Last Supper He broke the bread
The next day His blood was shed.
He died for me and you alike
My Savior shines as a bright light.

On the third day He rose again
Just as He had told us when.
He rose again for me and you
He rose to fulfill the scriptures too
He rose again to be glorified
Now I know....why He died!

Oh Lord How Beautiful

Awakening in the early morning,
I sense the crispness, freshness,
The brisk thrill of the morning air;
The birds with their beautiful melodies,
Creatures beginning their day's work.
And what comes to my mind?
Oh Lord how beautiful!

As I prepare myself for your place of worship,
I can feel the calming internal peace that flows through me.
As I am conscious of your ever watching eyes,
I look upward at the cross in the front of our church,
A brief feeling of compassion enthralls me.
However, joy and love overcome this feeling as I say to myself,
Oh Lord, How beautiful!

An afternoon walk finds me gazing across
A vast area of fields, green grass bringing forth freshness unto
the world.
With a distant hillside placed in the background,
The pure white clouds in the distance seem to touch the hills
Seemingly bringing me closer to you.
Oh Lord, how beautiful!

How many times dear God have I told you that I love you?
But still it does not seem like I tell you enough.
How many times have I asked you to forgive me?
Oh Lord, it seems like too many!
Our love cannot match yours,
Our sins are covered by your blood
Oh Lord, How beautiful!

At night I stare into the skies,
Heavenly bodies suspended in an infinite space.
Are you there God?
Are you among your beautiful creations?
The stars seem to ask so many questions;
I cannot answer them.
Only You know the answers.
There is nothing to match the beauty of the night skies.
Oh Lord, how beautiful

My prayers include many people, many things
In my prayers I wonder when you are coming back.
I wonder about-heaven, Lord.
Oh Lord, please show me how beautiful

Out of my Comfort Zone

D id you ever find yourself face to face with a situation you knew would take you out of your comfort zone? Perhaps you sought any reason or rationalization to help you avoid such a situation, even though at the time you knew it might be the right thing to do.

While in the Dominican Republic on a missions trip, I experienced such a comfort zone challenge. Now, I would describe myself as a somewhat quiet, reserved, and never wanting to draw attention to myself individual. As I was preparing to leave home for the trip (itself a comfort zone challenge), I knew ahead of time that our team would be involved mostly in construction, but there would be a day of local ministry. As I prayed, I wholeheartedly told the Lord that I would do whatever He needed or wanted me to do. I also asked that I would be a blessing to all that I came into contact with—I wanted to surrender totally to His will.

The construction phase went well and was very productive. As the day of ministry came, we were to go to a local school and minister to the children in various ways—songs, skits, dance, and games. As we prepared to go to the school, the call for three volunteers to dress as clowns was announced. Younger children seem to be receptive to clowns during the ministry presentation. Being one of the more reserved, older members of the team, I had no intention of volunteering, especially when I found out that the clowns were to be part of a group dance during the skit for the kids. NO. NOT ME — thank you!

Two volunteers came forward immediately—of course they were much younger and probably had done this type of thing before. When the call came again for the third clown, no one responded. My friend yelled out, "Sam will do it." I admit that I was a little upset. I did not "sign on" for that—so I thought.

I departed the room and went outside to the patio. The estate was surrounded by mountains, and it appeared as though I could reach out and touch them. One of my favorite scriptures, Psalm 121: 1-2, came to mind, and the words seemed to be alive as I gazed upon the beautiful mountains in front of me. "I will lift up my eyes unto the hills, from whence comes my help. My help comes from the Lord, who made heaven and earth." I pondered these words. I cannot say that I have actually ever heard an audible voice from God. I believe I heard that "still, small voice". The impression was clear. My heart was impressed to the point I thought I was hearing God; "What if I need you to be a clown?" I remember responding audibly— and I am not proud to say this—"Trust me, you don't." Then the voice asked, "didn't you tell ME that you would do whatever I needed or wanted"? I said, "Yes Lord, I did—I will be a clown."

So I went back inside, got my clown suit on complete with makeup, and our entire group proceeded to a local school. There were songs, skits, and a group dance for the kids. As a clown with graying hair and dance moves which could hardly be called dance moves, it was a wonder I didn't scare the kids away!

At the conclusion, our entire group formed a double prayer line and asked all of the teachers and kids just to walk through so that we could pray for them as they passed by. There were over one hundred kids all together, and from that number there was one of the middle school students who stopped in the line. He grabbed hold of someone's leg and hip and held on tightly—it was mine! At that instant I realized that the gesture of this young person was the Lord's way of saying thank you to me for being obedient. With all that was accomplished during the week, that moment was my "ah ha" moment.

Since that time I have tried to be more mindful and obedient in times where I feel the Lord is asking me to step out of my comfort zone.

The experience has helped me when I needed to draw courage to share my faith with others.

My missions trip to the Dominican Republic was my fourth such trip. Each time, the spirit of camaraderie with fellow workers is something that will not leave me the rest of my life. The satisfaction of knowing that we have been a help to others leaves me feeling blessed. When I go on these trips, I go to serve and to give, but inevitably I bring home so much more.

On the final night of our trip, the young people performed a skit of their own for our team. It was acted out to the song, *Thank you for Giving to the Lord.* At the conclusion, the two young people that we became closest to approached the three of us "old guys", grabbed hold tightly, and prayed one of the most sincere prayers that I have experienced. Another moment burned into my memory that has brought countless fond recollections. Knowing I got it right that time and I didn't miss out is a good feeling.

Years later, we are still friends, separated by thousands of miles. If I never see them again in this life, I still know that I helped to make a difference in their lives for the good—and we will get to talk about it in heaven!

I am really glad that I stepped out of my comfort zone!

The Whole Duty of Man

Have you ever said these words: "Honey, could you please just tell me what it is you want me to do? Please?" Some men may not be mind readers —I know this man isn't. We like to have clear direction so that we can go about accomplishing the mission at hand!

You may be familiar with the expression "the only thing we have to do in life is to pay taxes and die." Perhaps we could admit to feeling this way in a weak moment.

Surely our lives have a greater purpose and meaning, but what could this purpose be? In times of reflection and self evaluation each of us has asked that very question. Certainly we are more than merely existing, taking up space and time. Wouldn't it be helpful to know what is expected of us and to have a path mapped out so we could know what we should be doing in the lives with which we are blessed?

In Ecclesiastes 12:13 it says, "Let us hear the conclusion of the whole matter: fear God, and keep His Commandments: for this is the whole duty of man." (Women too!). On the surface this seems simplistic, but it carries an enormous responsibility and far reaching consequences. At the same time it offers a clear way to understand what God wants us to do in the time we have been given. Let's take a deeper look into this verse.

When the author of Ecclesiastes says, "let us hear the conclusion of the matter," it seems to indicate that what we are about to be told is the result of an extensive search for answers. Boys and girls, it boils down to this, so to speak, so listen up; what you are about to be told is critical!

Duty—by definition —is something that binds us by a natural or moral obligation to do or perform; to do what is required.

A concordance will give a multitude of references to the fear of God or the fear of the Lord. To fear God is to give deference to His authority in all matters, to revere His majesty and give Him the honor due. He is the Creator of the universe, a Father, a friend, a helper, and a burden taker. He created the universe and man to attest to His glory (Genesis chapter one and Psalm 8:5-6). He is a Father to the fatherless (Psalm 68:5), a friend (John 15:14-15 and James 2:23), a helper (Psalm 54:4), and a burden taker (Psalm 55:22).

With this fear of God comes wisdom (Psalm 111:10), and knowledge (Proverbs 1:7). We will find these helpful to implement the Commandments in our everyday lives. The fear of God also brings blessings (Psalm 112:1). Sounds like a pretty good benefit package.

Wisdom is defined in the Funk and Wagnalls dictionary as "the power of true and right discernment," a valuable tool as we navigate choices to be made in school, work, and relationships. It goes on to say that wisdom will lead us to the course of action dictated by our discernment. Additionally wisdom helps us to exercise good, practical judgment. Wisdom will enable common sense. I would like an extra large scoop of that please!

Knowledge is more than just an accumulation of facts stored away in the recesses of our minds. Referring to the same dictionary, knowledge is information or understanding acquired through experiences. Maybe a reference to the "school of life" could apply here? The experiences we encounter in life will, in many instances, be determined by the choices we make. The definition goes on to say a practical ability or skill; again, many of which are determined by choices. Can we infer fearing the Lord will lead to good choices in life? Finally, knowledge is defined as a clear and certain apprehension of truth for a bit. How beneficial it is to have that apprehension of fact, subject, and truth! Hold the thought of apprehension of truth, for a bit.

We all want blessings, right? Blessings are those which makes one happy or prosperous, a gift of divine favor. Neat! Yet another product from the fear of the Lord! Deuteronomy chapter twenty eight, speaks of blessings. It says if we carefully observe God's Commandments, blessings will come. Actually, blessings will overtake us. We will find blessings from the fruit of our body (our children), blessings as we come and go in the city and the country. Our storehouses and all we set our hand to do will encounter blessings. We will be blessed to have our enemies be defeated!

We will find Commandments in both the Old and New Testaments. Most notably the Ten Commandments found in the Old Testament were guidance for us to know how to respect and honor God, and laws to keep us and society from hurt and destruction. I know, people think right away, "thou shall not, thou shall not, thou shall not," seems pretty restrictive. Perhaps it would be better to think of those Commandments as a guardrail instead of a confining fence—keeping us safe and avoiding destruction in our lives. God's Commandment is referred to as a lamp in Proverbs 6:23, being a light to guide and show us the way.

In the New Testament (Matthew 22:37-39), Jesus gives new Commandments—the "greatest Commandments" saying that we should love the Lord with all of our hearts, souls, minds; and secondly, that we are to love our neighbors as ourselves. Think about this for a minute. If these two commandments are truly followed, they render the others unnecessary and become defining guidelines for our lives. Verse forty of the same passage says that all of the law hangs on these commandments.

It is our duty to do what is right and just. The Commandments tell us that it is wrong to lie, cheat, or steal: to kill, covet, or to commit adultery. If we abide by the Commandment to love our neighbor as ourselves, we will not transgress upon our neighbor nor violate any of the other Commandments. Having society follow this Commandment would do what billions of dollars in prevention programs and billions more in police protection and prisons are unable to do.

We should not follow Commandments solely out of obligation. We should follow them because we desire to follow them. In Oswald Chambers' devotional, "My Utmost for His Highest," he writes, "The most important aspect of Christianity is not the work we do, but the relationship we maintain (with God), and the surrounding influence and qualities produced by that relationship. That is all God asks us to give our attention to, and it is the one thing that is continually under attack." We should not fear the Lord because we are afraid, but because we desire to know Him more.

In 1997, The Million Man March in Washington, DC was sponsored by the Promise Keepers organization. I and a few of my friends had the privilege of attending this massive rally. The movement is an attempt to help men find a way back to the guidelines that made individuals, families, communities, and ultimately society, good, productive and blessed. Promise Keepers is an organization which promotes family values encouraging, even challenging men to honor their duty concerning family; to be good, faithful husbands and fathers.

We speak of duty—to our family, our friends, our God. We would be wise to make duty a chief important in our lives. I do not believe that we are forced into compliance of duty. It is a choice and an opportunity as well. Matthew Henry, a great theologian of the seventeenth century, in his volumes of commentary asserts that in adhering to our "whole duty" we can find true happiness, and attain our great end.

Should we choose to seek out the whole duty of man? It seems we will reap multiple benefits. Who would reject wisdom, knowledge, and blessings? Earlier I asked you to hold the thought about apprehension of truth. Could it be that through the fear of God, as we gain wisdom and knowledge, we are led to the understanding of who God is? What He means to us? What He desires for us? As we come to the apprehension of truth, I believe we can find THE TRUTH! Jesus said in John 14:6, "I am the way, the truth, and the life: no man cometh unto the Father, but by me."

Through the fear of God we can gain a glimpse, and ultimately experience what God means in 1 Corinthians 2:9, where it says "But as it is written, Eye hath not seen, nor ear heard, neither have entered into the heart of man, the things which God hath prepared for them that love him."

SOUNDS LIKE A DUTY TO PURSUE!

Recalculating

Oh no—I missed the turn! An unscheduled and lengthy detour was my fate. The sometimes pleasant, but often irritating voice of the GPS was quick to point out my error. Most likely we will all have this experience while driving. As an error is made, the pronouncement "recalculating" informs us that a correcting path is about to be forthcoming.

How many of us have taken a wrong turn in life? Many times it is easy to correct our mistake and get back on the right track without losing much time or with little consequence. However, other times our wrong turn will lead to a long and maybe difficult detour in life. In Jeremiah 29:11-14, we are told the Lord has plans for us, and those plans are for good —to prosper and not to harm us —plans that will give us hope and a future. Ideally we would stay on course and not deviate from those plans, but because of our God given free will, we get side-tracked and often find ourselves on an alternate route in life. Can we get back to what the Lord's plans are for us? Yes. Is it always without heartache or consequence? Not always. But, we can get back on a good path moving forward.

Pastor Woodson Moore was my pastor for nearly forty years. I would hear countless sermons during this time—all meaningful and helpful. One in particular always had extra special meaning to me. About two years before he went on to glory, I remember telling him that my favorite sermon was the one he titled "Recalculating." Soon thereafter, he mentioned that sermon to the congregation and told them that I had indicated that it was my favorite. He then said, "I think that is my favorite one as well!" The words and meaning of that message will be forever in my heart.

In a nutshell, Pastor spoke of how we all make decisions and choices that determine our path forward in life, and sometimes these choices are not in our best interest and can be detrimental. The Lord will always make a way of escape for us to get back on His path. He is in the recalculating business!

"Recalculating" struck a chord with me because I have made some poor choices in life. I got off the planned road the Lord had for me, and I needed a recalculation. When I was a young man just out of college I believed I knew my immediate path forward. I planned to use my teaching degree to teach young people in middle school math and science. Early in the summer following graduation I met a young lady who turned my head, as they say. We decided to get married at the end of that summer—not having to, just decided to. Although she was a new Christian, the choice I made would prove to be a poor one. I secured a teaching position in a nearby town. It was not the ideal job in a school with split sessions with me teaching in the afternoon and early evening. I really was not happy there. My in-laws had a family business which they wanted me to join. Additionally, they were an important part of an up and coming evangelistic ministry—one of which I would become involved.

So within the first year I resigned my teaching position and became involved with the family business and the new ministry. I truly believe that my heart was in the right place as far as the ministry was concerned, but this too would soon prove to be a mistake. To make a very long story a little shorter, within five years my marriage would be over. My first wife basically decided that she did not want to be married any more.

Talk about getting out of the plans of the Lord! Within two years of graduating from college, I had abandoned my teaching career, chosen a woman to marry that was out of God's Will for my life, entered and exited a ministry that I should not have been a part of. Boy, did I make a wrong turn! I had made several poor choices which altered the course of my life.

The divorce was civil and I remained friends with the family. We had no children together. By the end of the five year marriage (on paper anyway), I was immune to a broken heart because of the circumstances, but I did sense my "torn spirit." I felt like a failure. The Scripture says "the two shall become one flesh." When the one flesh is torn apart, I believe there is a tearing of our spirits. Healing will come, but scars will remain.

I needed the Lord's help. I remember the months following the separation as one of the loneliest, most difficult periods of my life, even though what had transpired had to be. Sometimes we just cannot have control over a situation.

Throughout my life there were times that I would journal extensively—especially when things were going rough, and this was one of those times. During this time I had what I call an "Elijah moment." In 1 Kings 19:4, Elijah had become so discouraged he wanted God to take his life. As my loneliness continued, I would journal similar sentiments. One day in particular I wrote, "Lord I can't take this anymore. If you don't have someone for me, please take me." Psalm 139 asks the Lord to "search me," and the word used for search refers to probe. God will know our depths. I felt alone, but I knew better. I knew the Lord was with me, and I am sure He knew my depths at that time.

It is sad that statistics show that a high percentage of marriages end in divorce. Even sadder is that the percentage for Christian couples is roughly the same. I am in that statistic. Of course the Lord hates divorce. I have come to realize over the years that divorce is not the unpardonable sin. If we have experienced this, the Lord can and will forgive and set us on a new path. Sometimes things can't be overcome. If a partner chooses to be unfaithful or abusive or chooses not to love anymore, the path forward in such a marriage is very difficult.

I remember wondering about the scripture in Romans 8:28, where it says "All things work together for good to them that love God." Would my situation EVER work for the good? Now of course God does not cause bad things to happen to us. I believe this passage means that even out of bad things that happen, God can cause good to come from them.

Not long after, I met my wife Sherry for the first time. Some mutual friends had planted the seed saying maybe I should call her, and by some coincidence she was attending one of two churches I was attending at the time. I was twenty eight years old but felt as nervous as a teenager making that first call. Of course I still remember the date as July 16, 1983. During a brief five minute talk, I asked if she would be interested in going out sometime. She said yes, and shortly thereafter we said our good-byes. I waited a whole five minutes before calling her back asking what was she doing that night! Sherry happened to be free so we decided to drive to the Ocean City boardwalk in New Jersey. We strolled for nearly four hours as we talked and shared so many things.

We had not been total strangers. Actually we went to the same high school only one grade apart. Interestingly, she had been a cheerleader cheering for my wrestling matches, so she knew then who I was. Honestly, I suppose I was aware of her in high school, but had no recollection of any meetings.

As the evening progressed, we shared about our very similar hurts from a failed marriage, each having ended after about five years. Each of us confided that —if honest—we knew we should not have entered our perspective marriages, but did so anyway. It was a great time of sharing and walking the boards at the ocean's edge on a beautiful summer night. Perhaps oddly, the feeling I remember most was how wonderful it felt just to be with someone who actually wanted to be with me. The next day we attended church together and went to the beach in the afternoon. Life seemed good!

A week later we had another date, and the relationship was blossoming. Our mutual faith was so important. Sharing common experiences and circumstances we quickly discovered we had several mutual friends we were not aware of initially. Both of us were schooled to be educators of math. Our similarities continued and were almost unbelievable.

We married about two years later—now thirty-seven years ago. With three grown married daughters, and seven grand children, the Lord has blessed us immensely. Over the years I have looked back on that first date, and have to admit, it was my best day! Have you ever had something happen to you where you thought it was too good to be true—but it **was** true? Can you identify your best day? Had it not been for that day it is possible none of the ensuing blessings would have manifested. My wife always says, "The Lord is the master chess player." I liked His move on that day!

If we could imagine our life path, and we look back to see where we have been, undoubtedly we will see turns off the main route, forks in the road, maybe some smooth road, bumpy terrain, bridges, and even mountains and valleys we have traversed in life. Every time we got off the main path, (the "good plans" from Jeremiah chapter twenty nine), I believe God's recalculating was already taking place.

As the Scripture says our mourning will be turned to dancing. Psalm 30:11 says, "Thou hast turned for me my mourning into dancing; thou hast put off my sackcloth, and girded me with gladness." Our brokenness and our ashes will be replaced by beauty, and we will be renewed. (Isaiah 61:3). Sins can be forgiven. We will once again be on the good road.

I wrote earlier of my "Elijah moment," when Elijah cries out and wanted to have his life taken, and I myself had felt the same way. Well, Elijah did not die. An angel came to give him food and caused him to rest so that he could go on. My prayer was heard as well. I also previously mentioned how I would journal often, especially in my low times. Ten years or so after Sherry and I married, I came across my journal from my lowest period—checking the dates, I was astonished to find the date I had asked the Lord to take me if things were not going to change. The date was July 15, 1983, only one day before I called Sherry for the first time! I have said publicly on more than one occasion that Jesus

Christ saved my soul and Sherry Simmerman saved my life! Proverbs 18:22 says he who finds a wife finds a good thing. The Lord recalculated for me —and I found a good thing!

No matter where you are in life's journey, young or old, if you are out of God's plan for your life, the Lord can and will recalculate for you to get you back on the road He has for you. Be expecting and open to His leading. Have the courage and staying power to alter your course. Let a "recalculation" take place in your life!

Forgiveness Begets Forgiveness

It has been said that unforgiveness is a poison that we prepare for others but drink ourselves. The "ill" feelings we harbor for others often end up adversely affecting us, be it mentally, physically, or spiritually.

The Bible speaks many times of forgiveness. In Mark 11:26, it says plain and simple if we don't forgive we won't be forgiven; "But if you do not forgive, neither will your Father which is in heaven forgive your trespasses."

I never cease to be amazed by individuals or families who forgive an offender for unspeakable hurt —even the murder of a friend or family member. I know I would have to struggle to forgive in such a case.

Of course, there is a wide range of offenses that we encounter in our lifetime. There are times when we offer forgiveness and it is rejected. Other times we need to forgive even if the offending party will have no knowledge of our forgiveness because they are unreachable or may have passed. Regardless, we are told to do so.

I have written before concerning a family which was instrumental in my coming to the Lord at the age of sixteen. For the next two years I was made to feel as one of the family. I cherished the times we shared attending church activities, and discussing the Word of God as I was beginning my Christian walk. They showed me the love of Jesus in all that they did. I have always considered them my spiritual Mom and Dad.

In subsequent years I would stay in contact with my dear friends by an occasional card, note, or an infrequent encounter. There was a period of years where life was not the best. I struggled with the hurt from a failed marriage, the realization of a grave mistake by leaving teaching, and the consequences of poor decisions made concerning the direction of my life at that time. I became bitter and unforgiving of my first wife and circumstances involving her family.

As the years passed, I thought the bitterness and hurt had been suppressed and disappeared from my life. (So I thought). Fast Forward another thirty years. In that space, my spiritual Dad had passed on to Glory, but my spiritual Mom was still residing in the area. One day I worked up the courage to call and ask her to lunch. It was wonderful to see her again after so long. She was as special as always! During the next year we had the opportunity for a few lunches where we were able to catch up from the many years past.

On one such occasion, my heart could not help but open and share with her about the hurt I had experienced from my failed first marriage. In addition, sharing the shame I carried from poor decisions made as a result of my involvement with my ex wife's family. I hadn't spoken about that period of my life in many, many years, yet something compelled me to do so.

As "Mom" listened, I realized that I still harbored unforgiveness in my heart. Once again, the family that helped me so much as a young Christian, was now, more than forty years later, guiding me again in my spiritual walk. I knew that I needed to get the bitterness from my past behind me for good. Taking some reminders from that period of my life, I placed them in the fireplace. In my mind and heart, I ceremoniously displaced all of those ill feelings. I had envisioned placing items in the fire—watching them burn slowly from page corner to corner (like in the movies), but the instant I placed them in the fire—it was like spontaneous combustion —a big "poof"—-and all of the materials were gone in an instant.

About a week after my "burning ceremony," I received a call from a previous client for whom I had done work. They called me to list their home for sale. The wife explained that the reason they needed to sell was because her husband was terminal. So, on the appointed day, I stopped to review the paperwork with them. As I was leaving, the wife followed me to my car, and tears began to fill her eyes. She told me that her husband had accepted his fate, but was not ready spiritually. She said he still carried bitterness and unforgiveness toward his ex-wife and her family for hurting him. Really? She also told me that her husband wanted someone to talk to about this, and to pray with him. Additionally, he would be willing to talk with ME only. Again, really?

I immediately realized this was the very same issue I had just come to grips with in my own life—just a few weeks prior. I remember telling the wife, "I have just the story for your husband!" I met with the husband two times. I was able to share my story of unforgiveness, and how, forty years later, I finally let go of my bitterness. This helped open his heart. I was able to pray with him about his feelings from the past. We read scriptures together. My friend then gave his heart to the Lord. He passed a few weeks later, but I know that I will see him again someday.

I believe I was afforded this opportunity because I had just extended forgiveness myself. God says His Word will not return to Him void. His Word—even command—to forgive, became real in my heart, and in turn, that Word brought forgiveness to my friend's heart, and salvation to his soul.

To forgive can be a daunting challenge. However, the ensuing freedom it brings can be, as they say—PRICELESS!

Life Lines

I have never visited a palm reader. My imaginations as a youth at the carnival or county fairgrounds of the palm reader's booth were a semi lit area where one would sit down at a table to have the reader tell my future. I imagined a candle on the table, curtains all over the walls and ceiling, and some mystic grabbing my hands, looking at my palms, and telling me about my life—past, present, and future. Supposedly one's told about marriage, finances, peace or trouble ahead. Um — no thanks!

As I began to write this story I decided to research palm reading for some background information. I have to say, just being on the search page with numerous links to reading palms felt creepy. I did not stay there long, but gleaned palm reading as an attempt to identify personality characteristics, predict future happenings, and interpret the meaning of our palm lines and how they intersect or not. Enough said. Too much actually!

Personally I have always been intrigued by thoughts and discussions concerning how our lives intersect (or not) with others. Specifically how such an encounter coincidentally—or perhaps Providentially—could alter the course and outcome of another person's day or life.

When we look at our palms we see lines. Some intersect and some do not. These lines referred to as life lines make me think of people in my own life, and how we met and came into the relationships we did. A couple of years ago my wife and I went to dinner with two of our dear friends who came into our lives by interesting circumstances, and how our meeting has transpired to become the meaningful friendship it is today.

I have been accused of being a sentimental sap at times. After dinner I began to talk (it actually might have ended up more like a speech). When I look back on that talk, I sometimes get embarrassed a little. I described in detail how each of them, including my wife, crossed my path—- my life line in a specific instance. The initial encounters may have seemed to be by chance or even insignificant at the time but were actually a defining moment in our relationships.

I find it interesting to read in Isaiah 49:16, where God says, "Behold I have graven thee upon the palms of my hands." Of course God knows us (He made us), but what is the significance of being "engraved" on His palms? The Matthew Henry commentary says by engraving us on His hands He is saying we become a seal upon His heart, and that He is always mindful of us and our interests. Where we might need to tie a string around our finger or hand to remember something, God will never need to do so because we are engraved in His hand!

My all time favorite movie is *It's a Wonderful Life.* I could list many life lessons learned from this movie. It is a sad scene when George Bailey bemoans "It would have been better if I had never been born." Clarence the guardian angel goes on to show George how the lives of others would be so different without him. Clarence's statement rings so true. "Every man's life touches so many others."

There are many ways that we get to touch others. It could be as simple as an uplifting word to a stranger, a deed, a small gift. I came across an interesting post recently (author unknown) that said, "You might think that you don't matter in this world, but because of you, someone has a favorite mug to drink their tea out of that you bought for them, or read a book you recommended that brought them pleasure." An encounter we have could be day changing or life altering. Have you ever been told that you "made my day"? You never know.

As the Lord has engraved us on His hands, He knows our comings and goings, the people we will meet in life, the opportunities we will have to bless others, and what we will do with those opportunities. Jeremiah 29:11 says, "For I know the plans I have for you, declares the Lord, plans to prosper you and not to harm you, plans to give you hope and a future." (NIV) I believe we can be prospered by the people we meet in life and the effect they could be on us; and we can prosper others by crossing their life lines as well. We might be tempted to immediately think of prosper in a financial light, but prosper also means to thrive or flourish. This is God's plan for us, and I believe that people we meet are part of that plan. I believe that we can help others to thrive and flourish by things we say or do for them.

My father and mother met by chance at a roller skating rink which was in a town different from either of their respective home towns. If they had not met, you would not be reading this story. Coincidence or Providential? I choose Providential. Think of this (because I do all the time), and this would be similar for you and your family as well— had they not met, gotten married and had me, then my wife would be married to someone else, our children and grandchildren would not be alive, and only God knows the entire ramifications of my mom and dad's meeting. Not small potatoes in my opinion.

All of our choices and actions have consequences, but we cannot get bogged down in worry about making future decisions or in guilt from past decisions. When we pray, we should ask God for guidance and to show us the way. Proverbs 3:5-6 says, "Trust in the Lord with all thine heart; and lean not unto thine own understanding. In all thy ways acknowledge him, and he shall direct thy paths."

Will our steps be coincidental? Or by divine appointment? Our steps will certainly have a ripple effect as we touch another life, and they in turn touch others.

Two years ago, my current Minister, Pastor Ken showed a video in church which began by showing one person giving an uplifting word to another, who then came to church and accepted the Lord; who then went to work and witnessed to others—one of which sought a different career because of this witness, then started a business where many were blessed....The ripples continued until the end where we see the last person crossing paths with the person who started the video. The caption read "And they never knew" meaning the last person would never know it was the first person who started the chain reaction as their life paths just crossed. (Hope I did not lose you here) I told my pastor "That was cool, but I believe that someday in heaven we will get to know all those involved in helping us get to where we are in life." Just sayin'.

My friend Steve has a heart for missions. He has been on over fifty trips around the globe. Many of his trips are with an organization called Builders International, whose motto is "We go to places where no one else wants to go." Steve has many stories of people being helped and having their lives and communities changed because of the faithfulness of this group.

One story in particular is where an individual came to Christ and over time started churches throughout his country. Steve and his companions saw a changed life that is bringing changes to an entire country. Steve seeks no credit for himself, but because of his willingness to go— to have his life line cross paths with other lives—people are having their eternity changed! It is cool to think about all of the life lines Steve has crossed in the world. The day in which the number of souls reached are tallied from his and his organization and many others like it, will be a glorious day for sure!

We have many opportunities before us in this life. We don't have to travel to a foreign mission field to find a place where we are needed. At times we might be the only person to cross paths with someone in need. Now please stay with me when I say this: We cannot help in EVERY situation. However, when we do feel impressed to help in some way—as the Holy Spirit prompts us —we should do our best to help. It has been said that "No one can do everything but we all can do something." There have been times in my life when I missed it. I would tell my wife later, I knew I should have stopped to help or give a word, but I did not. It is not a good feeling to know you missed it. I have to ask forgiveness and ask the Lord to help me know for the next time. We never know when our life line encounter could become a "lifeline" to someone.

Random acts of kindness, a timely card, or a small personal gift can go a long way in making our "life line crossing" a meaningful event for someone. Maybe we will get to see the impact now. Maybe we won't see the impact until we get to heaven.

Finally, there are individuals who have crossed our life line and perhaps altered our life for the better in some way. If we have not told them already how appreciative we are, then we should tell them. If there are things we would say in memory, gratitude, or honor of someone, let's not wait until the funeral to do so. These things are worth saying right now to them. Please do so. You won't be sorry.

Always know you have an impact on people. As our life lines cross, we have fingerprints – DNA— on each other that can never be wiped away!

We Wrestle Not
Holding On...

For we wrestle not against flesh and blood, but against principalities, against powers, against the rulers of darkness of this world, against spiritual wickedness in high places" (Ephesians 6:12)

During times of personal struggle, I sometimes think back on my days as a high school wrestler. Wrestling, for the most part, is an individual sport which is a battle of strength, quickness, and mastery of various moves. I faced many opponents who were stronger or quicker, all of whom were very eager to subdue me. One reason for my continued success was my ability to control my opponent with holds that controlled his wrists and ankles. This prevented him from taking the offensive and initiating attacks against me. By holding on with all my might, I could control someone who was stronger and quicker than I was.

Inevitably we will encounter battles that will test our resolve. "Mountains" will need to be climbed and overcome—or moved. Sometimes our battles will not be resolved immediately. Sometimes the mountains are not climbed in a single day. During times of delays; real or perceived—what should we do? What hold would be an effective weapon?

In my early Christian walk, I remember, Matthew 17:20, which says if we have faith as a grain of a mustard seed, we could speak to the mountain and it would be removed... thinking a literal mountain would physically move. I came to believe that mountains are more like a roadblock—a deterrent of some sort—- to keep the Will of God from manifesting in my life. The scripture above in Ephesians 6:12, says we wrestle against "spiritual wickedness in high places... and the rulers of darkness of this world." The battles are real and sometimes take quite an effort to overcome such a formidable foe.

In our spiritual struggles, we sometimes find that in order to achieve victory we must hang on for dear life. Ephesians 6:13 tells us to put on our full armor of God so that we can "stand our ground." It continues by saying that after we have done everything to stand...stand firm! Should we infer from this that we might have to stand further even if we are doing everything we can to stand at some point—because sometimes the battle continues even after we are standing?

Using the "holds" God has shown us enables us to prevail. The prayer of faith is one such hold. In James 5:15 we read, "And the prayer of faith shall save the sick, and the Lord shall raise him up; and if we have committed sins, they shall be forgiven him."

Our faith might require some action to climb our mountain or free us from the roadblock or deterrent that we face. Our faith may require an action that may be considered more of a passive action, like laying our burden at the feet of Jesus? Sounds easy, right? For some perhaps, but for others not so easy. Either way we are told to do so. In Psalm 55:22, we are told to "Cast your burden upon the Lord, and he shall sustain you; he shall never suffer the righteous to be moved." We MUST grasp, that by letting go we are using a weapon against our enemy—our opponent. We also must realize that we cannot do everything in and of ourselves. We need to be humble before God by acknowledging how much we need Him! Entrusting Him to our cares and burdens is not a sign of weakness, but of strength! I believe God knows this too, and why He tells us to cast our burdens upon Him. As we release our concerns, our faith muscles will be strengthened and become an effective hold against the enemy.

The good fight of faith helps us to lay hold of the coveted goal. "Fight the good fight of faith, lay hold of eternal life, where unto thou art also called, and hast professed a good profession before many witnesses." (1 Timothy 6:12).

Finally, God's promises are "effective holds", because if we are in Christ, the promises of God are ours. "And if ye be in Christ's, then are ye Abraham's seed, and heirs according to the promise." (Galatians 3:29) In 2 Corinthians 1:20, we are told that God's promises are "Yes and Amen"! In Numbers chapter twenty three, it says that God cannot break a promise. He is not a liar.

The promises of God are numerous. Each of us would be well served to do a search of them and keep them handy for future reference. These promises can be read and applied when we encounter trials or circumstances where we feel as if we need to hang on for dear life.

The following is a small sample of such promises:
Eternal life through Salvation: John 3:16
Strength: Isaiah 41:10 and Psalm 46:1
Forgiveness: I John 1:9
God is with us in dark times: Psalm 23
He will never leave or forsake us: Hebrews 13:5
Peace: John 14:27 and Philippians 4:7
Safety: Psalm 27:5
Unfailing Love: Isaiah 54:10
His plans for us: Jeremiah 29:11

God's promises need to be an anchor for us in times of trials and trouble.

Over the years as I reflected on the analogy of the wrestling holds to our spiritual holds, I thought of the holds as a defensive tool. While in the midst of a recent trial, a friend posted a quote by Christian author, J. R. Miller, which in essence says through holding on and standing firm while not losing hope, victory can be won! Sometimes it is much harder just to wait and hold on. The scripture says when we have done all to stand— if the victory isn't won yet, then we need to stand some more! Perhaps holding on is really an offensive weapon at our disposal and not a passive defensive one? Maybe by holding on we are actually fighting through and paving the way to the final victorious resolution to our trial.

By hanging on with the prayer of faith and promises of God, we will obtain the victory that is ours if we persist. Our battle may be for a physical problem, personal, financial, or the burden for a lost loved one. We are in a constant battle against the things of the world that try to subdue and gain victory over our lives. When the time of battle comes, we can be prepared to use these spiritual holds to gain control and receive the victory. Whatever the battle, know that God is in control and is always there with us. He will see us through. Let's hang in there to the end and finish the match victoriously. "I have fought a good fight, I have finished my course, I have kept the faith." (2 Timothy 4:7)

Psalm thirty-six tells us that the Lord's faithfulness reaches to the clouds, and His love is steadfast! He wants us to hold fast onto Him as He holds fast onto us.

His Word Shall not Return Void

So I have a story to tell you. One that is personal and meaningful to me. I would like to share how the following passage became so real to me—how His Word ministered to my heart and "accomplished toward His purpose," and returned to me in a literal way.

We read in Isaiah 55:11 "So shall my word be that goeth out from my mouth; it shall not return unto me void, but it shall accomplish that which I please, and it shall prosper in the thing where unto I sent it."

I was raised in the Catholic Church, but by my early teens was no longer involved. When I was sixteen, I gave my heart to the Lord, asking Him to be my Lord and Savior. I have mentioned my "spiritual family" who helped me during that period of time. To say the family was special would be a gross understatement. During that time, they had given me a Bible, which I treasured for a decade and had planned to keep in my possession forever. (The Lord had other plans).

Now, one might be tempted to think—a Bible?—that's nice, but there are millions of Bibles purchased and given each year—what's the big deal? To me, this Bible represented a life change. It was given by a loving family in possibly the most impressionable two years of my life. It was special to me.

Years later, I was working in retail with a friend who always noticed my Bible on my desk. He would ask me questions about scripture. He was not a Christian at that time. One day he was injured at work and had to leave indefinitely. I knew he had been "searching." I felt compelled to give him my treasured Bible. So I did. I also knew that I would probably never see him again because of his plans to move out of the area. After he left, I had no contact with him—not knowing where he was, if he had a family, or if his injury had persisted.

One afternoon nearly thirty years later, I received a phone call where the voice sounded familiar but I could not identify the caller. It was my friend I had worked with so long ago and given my treasured Bible. He had seen my name and number on a real estate sign. He was back in the area. We talked for several minutes about the usual stuff—how are you, tell me about your family, what brings you back to the area.

Then I had the courage to say, "Now, I am not asking for this back, but… "He interrupted me in mid sentence. He said, "I know what you are going to ask. You are going to ask about your Bible that you gave me." He then said, "I know how important that was to you. I want to tell you something. I became a Christian. I carried your Bible everywhere. All of the notes you made were helpful and important to me." He went on to say that he had become a missionary, and ministered in the Dominican Republic and in New York City where he had lived for a long time. He added, "Your Bible is worn, but I took good care of it for you, and I want to return it to you now."

I thought that was pretty cool. God is cool! I thought it a cool coincidence that within a year prior to this call, I had returned from my first foreign missions trip – in the Dominican Republic!

I was blessed. His Word was LITERALLY returning. It had not been void of blessings, victories, and additions to the Kingdom because of my friend's faithfulness to speak the Word.

The remainder of the verse says…."But it (the Word) shall accomplish that which I please, and it shall prosper in the thing where unto I sent it."

God's Word had done just that. I am glad that the Lord used me—my Bible—as an instrument to help accomplish the things that He purposes! I believe that it will be rather neat to someday see how our words and deeds may have affected others that have crossed our paths, and how the Lord used these to minister to another, or many. Even things that were said and done with no conscious thought that they might be affecting anyone. I also believe that as others were blessed, and in turn bless others, that we will get to see the "line of blessings" that began with our words and deeds.

This sentimental boy feels blessed to have his Bible back again. I will hang on to it for the rest of my life – unless the Lord has other plans…AGAIN!

Who Gives this Woman?

Mothers of the Bride—please forgive me—there is no offense intended!

During a wedding ceremony— after a father walks his daughter down the aisle, he is normally asked……."who gives this woman to be married?" Traditionally, the father would answer—-"her mother and I."

Earlier on, the father would answer "I Do." According to one source, "I Do" might date back to when women literally belonged to their fathers who would marry them off in exchange for some dowry.

Now, as a father of three daughters, I never sought after any dowry. I did pray since each daughter's birth—for the right man—the man that the Lord would have for them—to come into their lives at just the right time. That he would be a man who would love and honor her and their children.

My wife and I have "given away" three daughters. When the first was married, I wanted to give them something that would be meaningful as well as a challenge to my new son-in-law. The following is what I felt impressed to write. It became a gift that I shared with each of the three daughters at their weddings. At our eldest daughter's wedding I was given the honor of reading this letter:

Who Gives This Woman
To Be Married To This Man...

I DO

Two small but powerful words. A man utters them in at least two life changing moments: when he takes his bride in covenant with her and God, and when he relinquishes his role as protector for a daughter and passes that role to the man she is to marry.

In passing that role to you, I am passing on a significant and profound part of my life. My daughter, my flesh, my gem. Years of nurturing and guiding. Years of joy, and sometimes tears. Times of reflection, cherishing the moments in which I made a profound difference for good in the life of my little girl, and reflecting, too, on opportunities missed to be the best dad that I could.

You've won her heart, and now your life should be spent in keeping it. This is an awesome responsibility.

1 Corinthians chapter thirteen, says that love is long suffering, patient, and kind. Love is not envious, nor does it boil over with jealousy. Love does not insist on its own way. Love always thinks the best of your life mate, and it bears up under anything that comes. Powerful words, that if adhered to, will reap a lasting and wonderful life together.

This scripture also says that even if we have all kinds of faith, give all we have to the poor, give ourselves as a sacrifice —and we don't have love —we are nothing. This is a difficult but rewarding challenge.

As head of the family, you are entrusted to be a leader. Many times the final decision will rest with you. However, there will be times when "your way" may not be the right way. A wife is placed by your side to give wise counsel. My prayer is that you have the wisdom and the courage to make the correct choices.

A man should never be so hard as to never shed tears. It is not a sign of weakness, but of tenderness and compassion. Nor is it a sign of weakness to ask for advice or help when needed. Quite the contrary; it is a wise man that seeks out counsel when necessary.

In *The Way of the Wild Heart,* by John Eldredge, the author describes stages of manhood as being boyhood, cowboy, warrior, lover, king, and sage. Boyhood, he says is a time of exploration and wonder. Think of marriage as a journey, and as you grow and "explore" together, your foundation will be established. The "cowboy" is full of adventures. May you have wonderful adventures together. As a "warrior," you will need to be strong and ready to fight the battles that will undoubtedly come to attack you and your marriage. As "lover," you can enhance the beauty of your relationship and strengthen the bonds between you. To be "king" will not mean to rule with absolute power, but to lead in wisdom with a servant's heart. Remember, next to you as king stands the "queen" that you married. And finally, the "sage." This stage comes from a multitude of experiences and is not attained overnight. Let every experience of your marriage be a life lesson to learn how to be a better husband and father.

Now as you take my daughter as your bride, be mindful of Ephesians 5:25, where it says for husbands to love their wives as Christ loved the church and gave Himself for it. In giving Himself, Christ always forgives, He forgets our transgressions, and loves unconditionally. Love your wife as you would love yourself, and you will gain the reverence that will make your life together joyful, prosperous, and full of blessings.

My wife and I decided ahead of time that instead of saying "her mother and I," I would just say "I Do," as the father, giving his daughter to the new man in her life. Thankfully, we have three awesome sons-in-law. We are a blessed family.

Many years ago, before we had children, my wife and I attended a winter retreat in Lancaster, PA.. One speaker was the Rev. Dick Foth. I still smile to this day as I recall his words in one of his messages. He said "Marrying off your daughter is like giving a Stradivarius to a gorilla!"

As a dad, forgive me if I am tempted to feel that way…but they are all terrific gorillas!

Complete In Him

Have you ever struggled to put a jigsaw puzzle together, wondering if all the necessary pieces were there? First step for me is to pour out all the pieces onto a flat surface, arranging all before me in clear view. Sometimes I find myself wondering——-are all of the pieces really here or are some missing? This sure looks like a mess—how will it ever come together? Where do I start?

When we are facing a crisis or dilemma, we often may find ourselves asking similar questions. We see the pieces of the problem scattered in disarray. Everything seems a mess. How in the world will things ever come together to resolve our situation?

However, as with the puzzle, all of the pieces are there. Check the box—it tells us how many pieces are included, so we trust that is the case. Similarly, as we deal with a crisis or a problem, we should know that through Christ we have all of the pieces we need. Through Him we are complete. In Colossians 2:10 it says, "And ye are complete in him, which is the head of all principality and power."

So what are these "pieces" that we possess? We know that we can pray——- asking anything of the Father. We have the shield of faith to quench the fiery darts that come against us. We have the love of God. It says in Ephesians chapter three, that His love surpasses knowledge—that we may be filled to the measure of all the fullness of God. (sounds like a lot to me). The Lord's leading in wisdom can show us how to put the pieces together. Reach out to friends and family for support and guidance as well. Let's not forget joy (I know, sometimes we don't feel like being joyful), but joy can be an important piece of the puzzle. Psalm 16:11, tells us the Lord will make known the path of life to us and fills us with joy in His presence.

As joy is a choice, so is the "garment of praise." Isaiah 61:3, tells us to put on this garment instead of a spirit of despair. We have to choose to put that on—sometimes hard to do, but it makes the puzzle more clear. Try it! In all thy ways acknowledge Him, and He will direct thy paths. Proverbs 3:5-6, tells us to ask the Lord to order our steps—He will show us how to put our puzzle together.

We might be tempted to give up on the jigsaw puzzle for a variety of reasons. We get frustrated and want to get up and walk away. God does not give up on us. He will not leave us. He promises that He will never leave us or forsake us.

The "work" on us had its beginnings as written in Psalm 139:13-17. He knew us before, and as we were knit in the womb. In Philippians 1:6, we are told to be confident that He began a good work in us and will carry it on to completion until the day of Jesus. All of us are special—unique souls. God made us for a purpose—He does a good work in us—He wants to help us put our puzzles together. Each of us has special gifts, talents, callings, or ministries.

So, we pretty much trust the puzzle box when it tells us that all of the pieces are there, and that the puzzle will be complete. We can trust God when He tells us that we are complete in Him—all the pieces are there. Philippians chapter four, tells us that God shall supply all our needs according to His riches in glory. I believe this verse means more than just financial needs. ALL means ALL! Financial, physical, emotional, "whatever" needs. He has the pieces to any puzzle that we need to complete.

I Thought I was Being Asked a Favor

We all probably have been asked, at some point, to do something we really did not want to do. Perhaps it made us feel uncomfortable or afraid. Possibly, we felt unqualified or simply put, we did not want to do what was requested.

This past Christmas I received a book from a dear friend whom I love as a sister. The title was *Have a Little Faith,* by Mitch Albom. The reason I was given this book, I believe, was rooted in a quote on the cover. The quote begins, "In the beginning there was a question. Will you do my eulogy?"

My friend knew my hurts from the past. I had a younger sister who, after a courageous battle, succumbed to cancer at the age of forty-four. The final weeks were very difficult. My sister was a fighter. She battled until she couldn't anymore. She would do anything for friends or family when she was healthy.

A week before she passed, it was very evident all her strength had left her. As I was about to leave, she looked at me and said, "Brother, is there anything I can do for you?" I could not believe my ears. Even in her last days she wanted to know if she could help ME! All I could do was to shake my head and answer, "No Sis, I am okay." She then asked me one of the most difficult questions I have ever been asked. "Will you do my funeral?"

Thoughts flooded my mind. I am not a minister, I can't do this, I am not qualified. Fear wrestled me for a moment before I finally said, "Yes Sis, I will." I wanted to do this "favor" because my sister asked me.

The service was about two weeks later. My sister Karen passed on September 13, 2001 —two days after the attacks on the World Trade Center buildings and the Pentagon. It was a difficult week for many people. Trying to process everything at that time in our country and dealing with the devastating loss of my sister was only possible because of my faith.

I did not officiate the service, but gave the eulogy in honor of my sister. I have said to my wife and a few others over the years that giving the eulogy was one of the hardest things I have ever done in my lifetime, but it might have been one of the best things that I have ever done. At the conclusion I felt an overwhelming peace– the kind of peace that could only come from God Himself—the peace that passes all under-standing. (Philippians 4:7)

In subsequent years—as I have reflected—I have realized how blessed I was to have the opportunity to give the eulogy. Giving no credit to myself, I count it as one of my finest moments.

So back to the quote by Mr. Albom…."In the beginning there was a question. Will you do my eulogy?" It goes on to say "As is often the case with faith, I thought I was being asked a favor. In truth, I was being given one." Without a doubt, I have come to the realization that my sister was not asking me for a favor—she was GIVING me one! The feelings and memories I carry with me from that day will stay with me and comfort me all the days of my life. The honor, I will always feel, was a favor given to me.

In life, we encounter times when we are asked to give an offering, a tithe, to volunteer for a cause or special need—- whether providing a meal or sending a note or card—whatever the task. Surely, it seems like a favor is being asked of us. In reality, we are being given a favor —the opportunity to give.. Paul says in Philippians 4:17, that he doesn't want gifts for himself, but "that fruit may abound to our accounts"—-that we would be blessed because of the gift.

One might think the workers in the vineyard in Matthew 20:1-16, were given the favor of work, but in reality, when we are called to work for the Lord, it is we who are being given the favor—His gift of eternal life!

Now, that's a pretty good favor!

The Conspiracy

The surf pounded as the invasion finally began. For years the would be invaders hoped to secure, infiltrate, and possess the new land. The initial landing took place in a secluded area, then over the years spread to many locations. What would be the result of this mass invasion? Would it ever be stopped or defeated?

The hope was that the invaders would be beaten back, unable to withstand the elements or the natives. The first winter the conspirators were nearly wiped out, but their resolve seemed to grow with each passing year.

The invaders were called Pilgrims. The "conspiracy" was their intent to establish a new land for religious freedom, and a land the Pilgrim loyalists, in future generations, would attempt to label a Christian nation.

The Pilgrim influence was widespread at one time. The "conspirators" infiltrated many areas of the new American government. They called themselves Christians, and they actually claimed to have fifty two of the fifty five signers of the Declaration of Independence sympathetic to their views. In subsequent years, the offices of President and Vice President, Senate, Representative, and even the Supreme Court Chief Justice, all would be infiltrated. The history books and personal journals of the founding fathers were altered to give a false impression, a definite Christian slant to the lives and beliefs of the men that would determine the course of America.

The infiltrated government set up an education system that established schools and colleges in the name of Christianity. The New

England Primer and McGuffy Reader had definite influence. Nearly all of the first one hundred or so colleges were established by those faithful to the Christian cause and were used to spread the conspiracy throughout the land. It is not known how the conspirators managed to promote those in the cause to positions of leadership in these institutions, nor how it was managed to have a primary curriculum using Christian values and beliefs as a foundation. Even the famed Liberty Bell would somehow be inscribed with scripture, that being Leviticus 25:10, "Proclaim liberty throughout the land unto all of the inhabitants thereof." No doubt a rally cry for the conspiracy!

The cause boasted sympathizers such as Abraham Lincoln. Schools, hospitals, towns, would all come to bare Christian names: St. Christopher's, St Paul's, Los Angeles (city of angels), Corpus Christi (the body of Christ). Esteemed colleges were infiltrated as well. Yale's presidents were ministers until 1898. Somehow Harvard adopted the motto, "For Christ and the Church", and Princeton's motto was "Under God's Power She Flourishes". How could this be? The list seems endless. There are confirmed reports of stone cutters overtaking the Supreme Court building and etching the Ten Commandments on the walls of the Court. The conspirators were dealt a blow when conservative Judge Roy Moore from Alabama was forced to remove a statue of the Ten Commandments from his courthouse. The locals complained that should people read the Ten Commandments, they might actually be influenced by them! Horrors! The Library of Congress and many state and private institutions all were to fall victim to scripture references to the Christian cause, having been etched forever in stone. Congress was persuaded that the phrase "IN GOD WE TRUST" should be inscribed on the currency of the new land.

The mid 1960's finally proved to be a turning point in the battle against these subversives. The law would ban God, prayer, and Bible reading from the schools. The "new found separation clause" would enable the government to be free from these Christians, even though there is no such phrase in the document labeled the Constitution. Those engaged still in the conspiracy would have all to believe that increases in crime, violence, teen pregnancies, drug use, failing grades, and lack of respect for authority coincided with the removal of God and the Bible from public school and the government, and that these increases were in direct relation to the effect of having removed their Christian values. Undoubtedly, this is an unexplained coincidence!

Today, revisionists are doing an admirable job rewriting the history books to eradicate all traces of the Christian conspiracy. However, there has been an attempt to return to the beliefs of the past. The "radical right" is trying to renew the conspiracy and would have all believe that the founding fathers were indeed of the Christian persuasion. There is a determined effort to repeat the propaganda that the government was founded and based upon Christian principles and values, and those values and principles, if adhered to, would bring about a better nation. The "radical right" hopes to return to the values they say were the basis of education, government, and the community. Their rally cry is "blessed is the nation whose God is the Lord," (Psalm 33:12), and (2 Chronicles 7:14), "…If my people, which are called by my name, shall humble themselves, and pray, and seek my face, and turn from their wicked ways: then I will hear from heaven, and forgive their sin, and heal their land."

Efforts to stifle the uprising continue. The battle goes on!

Author's Note:

I was preparing this article to be included in this book in 2022, but I originally wrote the above article in August of 1996. It has never seen the light of day, being stuffed away in a manila folder somewhere. It is included in this book because I believe it has become even more relevant today, if possible, than when I first wrote it.

Harvard (as mentioned above) announced recently in a national news publication, that the head chaplain of the college is an atheist. The public school system is rapidly moving forward with an agenda that diametrically opposes Christian values. Many States are mandating the teaching of Critical Race Theory-1619 Project positions instead of our history (not perfect by any means, but nonetheless

OUR history), that describes our beginning as a nation, the strength that has come from America being strong and good. Alex DeTocquiville, a French political thinker and historian from the nineteenth century, came to live in America to study our way of life. He once wrote that "America is strong because America is good, and if America ceases to be good, she will cease to be strong"...And this I fear, is exactly what the forces of evil desire.

The Great and Small of it All

When I was a junior in college many years ago, my professor showed a video in science class that left an impression on me—one that has stayed with me for forty-five years. The video opened showing a young man in a park just looking around at life (trees, animals, other people). Then the man looked to the sky, and the video panned upward to the clouds, then the atmosphere, space, planets, stars, solar systems, galaxies, and finally the expanse of the universe. In so doing, showing how vast and endless were our surroundings. I am reminded of Psalm 8:3, "When I consider your heavens, the work of your fingers, the moon and the stars, which you have set in place."

The video returned to the man in the park as a mosquito landed on his arm. The camera zoomed in to the insect just as it bit the individual. Suddenly we could see the skin cells, then the blood vessels, the circulatory system, organs, the brain cells, and the body in total harmony as each member performed the duty necessary for the man to sustain life. I remember thinking—the majesty of God's creation!

Psalm 139:14 says, "I will praise you because I am fearfully and wonderfully made. Your works are wonderful. I know that full well."

I do not remember the professor saying anything about "God's creation," just that our essence is but a small part of the infinite universe on one side, and the microscopic details on the other. How sad.

Every summer I have the opportunity to visit the New Jersey seashore. Inevitably, I find myself gazing over the vastness of God's ocean. I realize that what I see, being so immense, is but a minute portion of

God's creation. This is a humbling experience. Genesis 1:9 says, "And God said, let the water under the sky be gathered to one place, and let the dry ground…..and the gathered water he called the seas." In His greatness, God made the land, the sea, and the earth and its fullness. He made the planets and the solar system, the entire universe. Here I am—a man—a relatively small part of it all. Am I significant?

Sometimes it is easy for me to get caught up in my every day activities, my work, and my future plans. At times, I get so involved in what I am doing that I feel everything must rely on me—that I must control things or nothing will ever get done. Then I remember how I felt at the beach. At that moment, all the self made plans, the ones that I thought were so important, ones that needed all of my energy and time—seemed trivial.

While the things we do are important, we must never let them become **so** important as to blind us from our original purpose in God's Master Plan. "And God said, let us make man in our own image, after our likeness…So God created man in His own image, in the image of God created He him; male and female created He them." (Genesis 1: 26-27) We are the purpose of His creation, and are here because He called us to be. Psalm 139:13 says, "For you created my inmost being; you knit me together in my mother's womb." We have a purpose, and God will fulfill that purpose, being the most important of His creation, made for His fellowship. If we are wise, we will make the choice to love and serve Him.

We ARE significant, and we alone can choose to love and serve God—the real purpose of life. We do not have to be overwhelmed by His infinite creations—nor lost in them.

FOR WE ARE HIS CROWNING ACHIEVEMENT!

More Than Just Fishing

Henry David Thoreau wrote, "Some men fish all their lives without knowing it is not fish they are after." As I ponder this quote my memory flashes back to some of the best days of my youth on a variety of fishing experiences. A love for fishing developed at an early age and still continues in my later stage of life. How can a man go fishing and not know fish are what he is after?

In *The Way of the Wild Heart*, John Eldridge writes of the stages of manhood, the first two being boyhood and cowboy. As boys we want to be loved by our Dads, desiring their approval. Unfortunately, many boys grow up never knowing that love and approval. Statistics are through the roof showing boys without a father in the home are more likely to get involved with drugs, crime, have a deficiency in education, and divorce later in life. All of us need to know, no matter the circumstances, we have a Father in heaven who loves us, cares for us, and approves of us. He is there. Always. We need to find Him. Seek after Him like we would seek after the catch of a lifetime!

I remember feeling close to my dad when I was ten to fourteen years old. First because he helped me get involved with baseball, but mostly because of the fishing trips. He would take me and my brother and sister on a party boat in the Delaware Bay. It seemed like we went every weekend during the summer and into the early Fall. I loved it and could not wait! When I look back I cannot believe he did that—having to deal with three young kids, tangled lines, and all that goes with a fishing trip. Yikes! I do not remember ever being tired or bored if the fish were not biting so much. As I look back, I wonder was I fishing or experiencing the bond with my dad? Yes I liked to catch the fish, but I have no clue how many or how big the fish were I may have caught. I just remember the good times I had with my dad. Was I seeking his approval at times? Possibly, more like probably, as we engaged in an activity that he liked as well.

During those same years I have great memories of fishing along our local Maurice River with one of my baseball friends and his dad, who was my Little League coach. They would pick me up many Sundays and we would fish from early morning until dusk, mostly for perch. We had our poles in the water all day, but remember leaving them unattended most of the time. What I remember most about these trips were the times my friend and I spent exploring the river banks, up and down the cliffs and adjoining woods. I was fulfilling part of my cowboy stage as Eldridge writes, by our adventures together. Nothing like exploring, but we thought we were fishing?

Another fishing experience etched as clear as day in my mind, was when some of the neighborhood friends and I would ride our bikes a couple of miles to an area of ponds and streams. We always loved exploring there. We found an isolated narrow stream that herring would get into. Talk about "shooting in a fishbowl!" There were so many fish in a confined area. We never took our fishing poles on these particular trips, but we made spears from sticks we found and used these spears to catch our fish. So in addition to the cowboy / adventure stage, we were experiencing the next stage of manhood, that being warrior. As we speared these fish, were we in our early stages of learning to be the hunter / gatherer/ protector that we are called to be as men? Or, were we just fishing? At that time of course, I thought we were fishing.

Our church and school emblem is that of the Warrior. In education and spiritual matters our Pastor's and Board's mission is to train warriors for the living God. Undoubtedly we will have many battles to fight through in life. We will be called upon to support and defend our family in a multitude of ways. There will be attacks on our children, our marriages, and our faith. There will be mountains to climb – education, employment, careers, and hard times to endure. Our warrior training is an essential stage as men.

The most anticipated weekend over several summers would be my turn to spend the weekend on my grandparent's boat in Cape May, New Jersey. I loved everything about that time, as my brother, sister and I would get to sleep on the boat for two nights. During the days we would get to ride on the boat, fish, and simply enjoy the times, even if we were just walking around the docks. My grandparents were great people. The quality bonding time we shared with them was, as they say, price-less! Although we saw them often over the years, that weekend together was for me at an early age, a learning experience in how to treat your kids and grand kids. We were important to them as they shared their valuable time, their kindness, and their treasure with all of us…And I thought I was going there to fish!

I was able to partially return the favor to my dad when I purchased a small boat when I was in my fifties. We would fish for flounder in the back bays of the Jersey shore and crab in the creeks not far from my home. Then there were our church sponsored men's fishing out-ings where I would get to take him fishing. One of my most cherished photos is that of my dad and my sons-in-law on one such trip. I was so happy to share that time with all of them. I was making memories for sure. They may have thought they were just fishing!

In addition, my small boat has provided numerous memories fishing with my wife over the years. She loves being on the water. It is a great, relaxing time in the peace and quiet as we make memories together. I always let her catch the most and biggest fish! Seeing my grandchildren catch their first fish is a time of bonding that will last a lifetime. It is hard to believe that a simple fishing trip could yield expe-riences that can shape lives. Or is it? Oh, and it was fun, too!

You may be familiar with a version of the following quote: "Give a man a fish and he will eat for a day. Teach a man to fish and he will eat for a lifetime!" When Jesus fed the five thousand, along with the bread

He gave them a fish to eat that day. What He taught them enabled them to eat for a lifetime!

If you have had the blessing of an earthly father in your life, you are fortunate. Perhaps he taught you how to fish. Perhaps you bonded with him, and that translated into a lifetime of blessings because of what he taught you in life. If you never experienced that bond or never had a father to show you positive life lessons, please know that our Heavenly Father can fill that void. In Psalm 68:5, it says we have "A Father to the fatherless, a defender of widows, is God in His holy dwelling." (NIV)

He wants to make us ALL fisherman! In Matthew 4:19 and Mark 1:17, Jesus tells us to follow Him, and He will make us fishers of men. He will give us what we need for a day —each day. As we allow Him to teach us, we will be able to eat for a lifetime—eternity! Then as we share what we learn with others, they too can eat for a lifetime!

LET'S GO FISHING!

He Was There All the Time

As the disciples walked along the road, they were saddened and troubled by the events of recent days. Their thoughts centered around what had just happened, and what could have been, if only their friend had lived. Life seemed to be going so well. Their friend had brought joy and peace to all who knew him, and now, everything was changed.

After walking for some time, they were joined by a stranger. They did not notice where he came from, only that he was suddenly in their midst. The stranger entered into conversation, and as the disciples described how their friend had been taken, tormented, and finally murdered, he could see how despair had overtaken them.

The disciples wondered who this stranger was, why he was there, where he was going, and why he seemed so interested and concerned with the despair that had befallen them. Perhaps they thought it incredulous that the stranger did not know of the recent events.

Soon they stopped for supper at an inn, sitting in a corner away from the crowded main room. The disciples realized that this was no ordinary man. When the stranger blessed the food, the disciples suddenly realized that this stranger was indeed someone they had known in times past. As quickly as they realized who this man was, he was gone —vanished! The stranger who had walked with them and talked with them was indeed the lost friend who was taken, beaten, and murdered.

The disciples were indeed, on the road to Emmaus after Jesus had been crucified. As they wallowed in their grief, Jesus appeared to them.

As they walked in their troubled time, Jesus was there with them, and they did not even know it!

How much are we like the travelers, walking along in life, sometimes depressed, confused, lonely, or feeling we are at the end of our rope? In these times we should know that Jesus is right here with us, even if we do not see Him!

In times of trials, sadness, or loss, when we face monumental decisions, we need to know the one who cares, the one who can help, has promised to be here by our side.

The twenty-third Psalm tells us that the Lord is with us. In verse four we read, "Yea, though I walk through the valley of the shadow of death, I will fear no evil: for thou art with me: thy rod and thy staff they comfort me."

Certainly there will be times when we feel alone, but we are not. The Lord is with us in our mountain peaks of triumph, our plains of daily routine, and even through our valleys of trials, heartaches, and needs.

In Matthew 28:19-20, Jesus instructs and commands the disciples to go forth, teach all nations, baptize them, and observe all the things that Jesus commanded. He ends with another promise; "Lo, I am with you always, even unto the end of the world." Always means all, any, every, and the whole time!

When the travelers stopped for supper, they invited the stranger to stay with them. Jesus accepted, as He always will to each invitation. If we ask and open the door, He will always come in. (Revelation 3:20)

As their "eyes were opened" during the supper, they recognized Jesus. The words of Jesus made their hearts burn. When His Word becomes real to us and our eyes are opened, our hearts too, will burn within us. Our hearts will burn with the truth and knowledge that no matter what the situation, decision, or circumstances, He is always there.

HE. IS. ALWAYS. THERE!

Mission for Success

Guys like to fix things. Having survived in a household with my wife and three daughters over the years, I was reminded continually how differently the minds of men and women operate. To a man, it is as simple as A –B – C – and problem solved! Women, I am told, have minds that operate differently. Everything is intertwined and much more complex.

I once taught a Sunday School lesson where I laid out the foundation for what I believed could solve all of the world's problems in one lesson of forty-five minutes. If only it could be that simple. Let's think of it as a mission to solve all of the problems of the world. For this mission we will need soldiers. Who's in? Who is ready to enlist?

Remember the song *Onward Christian Soldiers*? The song lyrics say "Marching as to war." War? Yes war. The lyrics continue "Christ, the Royal Master leads against the foe." The foe is our adversary the devil. He is the enemy about us who would thwart our mission if he could. Make no mistake, we are at war. The mission is not without risk. Still in? Your mission – should you choose to accept—(I could not help the reference to *Mission Impossible* here) — has a good benefit package and eternal security guarantee to those who are faithful to the mission.

Our mission is not to promote a religion but a relationship to Christ, the Royal Master. Readers who are familiar with the *Star Trek* series, know that the guiding principle of the Federation is the Prime Directive. This directive is clear in forbidding Federation members from interfering in such a way as to alter the normal evolution of any society. As

Christian soldiers, we have no such directive. Part of our mission is to persuade the inhabitants of the land to follow Christ the Royal Master. The soldier is expected to infiltrate to the extent of being an agent of change for the better.

Each soldier is to be equipped with a sword as a weapon, which is the Word of God. (Ephesians 6:17) The sword has more than one edge which will serve as both an offensive and defensive weapon. (Hebrews 4:12) The offensive edge can cut away at layers of hardness of the heart and prepare the heart to receive and administer forgiveness. The Word will show the way to eternal life. The defensive edge of the sword will stand against the working of the foe.

So the mission before us is a daunting one for sure. You may be thinking by now that this writer is crazy. Copy that. First up for standard issue would be a ten-pack of commandments. Let's start with the "Big Ten" which are found in Exodus chapter twenty. Soldiers are to assist in making inhabitants of the land aware of the Commandments and offer instruction and explanation as necessary without imposing judgment. Some might think the Commandments were meant to weigh us down almost to the point of bondage, but that is not so. In Proverbs 6:23 we read "For the Commandment is a lamp; and the law is a light: and reproofs of instruction are the way of life." A lamp is a good thing to make our paths easier to see. The law is light to instruct us in the way of life and to expose any evil that may be lurking about us.

One may recall years ago, Judge Roy Moore from Alabama was in a battle to keep the Ten Commandments posted at a courthouse. The opposition was quoted as saying "The Commandments must be removed because if people see them, then they might act upon them, and this is not acceptable!"   DUH!

What person in their right mind would be opposed to: not being lied to, not being murdered, not having someone have an affair with their spouse? How terrible would it be if we did not have to hear foul and vulgar and blasphemous language? Is it too much to ask to respect one's father and mother or to have a day of rest?

The Commandments are for our benefit. The Scripture says in Deuteronomy 30:19, that life and death, blessings and cursing are set before us. We would be wise to choose blessings and life. The law is there to help us and guide us as we traverse this life and the territory of our mission. We need to be aware of the minefield and ambushes that await us if we are not compliant with the commandments

All soldiers must be equipped with a rule. Specifically, the Golden Rule. Matthew 7:12 says "Therefore all things whatsoever ye would that men should do to you, do ye even so to them: for this is the law and the prophets." Instruction to the soldier would be to make each individual encounter personal, while offering up encouragement, prayer, and instruction of help. Each should share the Christian soldier manual and show your commitment to Christ the Royal Master. It has been said that people don't necessarily want to "hear" our sermon (instruction on how to follow Christ), but they want to "see" our sermon—(how we are following Christ). We must be a good example. Individuals will know we are under the command of Christ by the love soldiers show for one another. We are told this in John 13:35.

The next major ration that is necessary for this mission is a full helping of Matthew 22:36-38. Here we find "Master, which is the great Commandment in the law? Jesus said to him, you shall love the Lord your God with all you heart, and with all your soul, and with all your mind…this is the first and great commandment…and the second is like it, you shall love your neighbor as yourself."

Is it too much to ask to love the Lord— Christ the Royal Master—-with all of our heart, mind, and soul? On the surface it does sound like a lot to ask, but once people see the Lord for who and all He is, they willingly will offer up their hearts.

Loving our neighbor as we love ourselves? Who could resist? Verse forty of this same passage goes on to say "On these two Commandments hang all of the law and the prophets." What could this mean? One thought is that if we obey these Commandments— the first and great one, as well as the second which is like it—then the law and the prophets will not be necessary, as all matters will take care of themselves.

Finally, each soldier will need a supply of salt and light. We are told in Matthew 5:13-16, that we are to be the salt and light of the world. Now, we know that salt acts as a preservative, and an enhancer of taste. Light serves as a help to guide the way as well as a means of exposing evil and dangers before us. Soldiers must remove the salt shaker from their supply and deploy it wherever possible. A soldier can have the biggest or most beautiful salt shaker, but if the salt is not dispersed, it will have no effect. The salt only will achieve its purpose when spread among the substances it was intended to influence. Additionally, if the soldier does not remove his light so that it shines bright for all to see, the light becomes useless as well.

The would be soldier is wise to hear, meditate upon, and adhere to the following words: Christ, the Royal Master is our friend—a friend to all. If you encounter an angry individual, return any anger with a soft retort. Proverbs 15:1 says, "A soft answer turneth away wrath: but grievous words stir up anger."

It is becoming more and more certain that you will encounter individuals who will be offended by your message and will attempt to keep you quiet. Be reminded and gain strength from soldiers from an earlier era. In Acts 4:16-17, Peter, John and others were talking of Christ, the Royal Master and his good works when those in authority tried to silence them. Authorities said "What shall we do with these men...let us severely threaten them so they will speak no more." That didn't work! Later, Peter and John were thrown in prison—but they miraculously escaped! Still frustrated, the authorities had Peter and John beaten and told them to get out of town and don't speak of Christ anymore. That didn't work either! Today, prison for those soldiers who spread the Word is out of the question in our society, right?

Many soldiers have given their lives over the generations because they would not keep silent or would not recant their following of Jesus. Fox's *Book of Martyrs,* is a volume of instances where fellow believers were tortured and killed for their belief in Christ. Deitrich Bonhoeffer was a pastor and professor in Nazi Germany in the 1940's. He said "Silence in the face of evil is evil itself…Not to speak is to speak. Not to act is to act." Bonhoeffer, just weeks before the end of WWII, was hanged because of speaking out against Hitler. In Acts 4:29 it says "And now, Lord, behold their threatening: and grant unto thy servants, that with all boldness they may speak the word."

Ephesians 6:18 says "Praying always with all prayer and supplication in the Spirit, and watching thereunto with all perseverance and supplication for all saints." We must keep watch while on our mission.

Remember, as a soldier you are an ambassador for Christ. All actions must be done in love. The song says "what the world needs now is love, sweet love," and since God is love (1 John 4:8), we can infer that the world needs God.

The influence we seek to bring about cannot be forced. It is a choice for each to accept or reject. Hearts will have to change to achieve total and complete victory, and it is Christ and the Holy Spirit that are tasked with such an honor. Each soldier would be wise to heed the words of the prophet Micah, where, in chapter six, verse eight, he asks what the Lord requires of us. We are told simply to do justly, love mercy, and walk humbly with our God. If done, the mission will be a success!

Mission Accomplished!

If You are Reading this, You may be in Trouble

One of the sports I participated in while in high school and college was wrestling. More than one gymnasium where I competed had a sign affixed to the ceiling above the wrestling mat which read something like this: If you can read this sign, then you are in trouble—you are about to be pinned!

I never wanted to be able to read such a sign. However, there were times that I got a glance at the sign on the ceiling. I was on my way to trouble because my opponent was trying to pin me.

Perhaps, at times, even in our Christian walk, we find ourselves in trouble, down on "the mat of life." Our adversary, the devil, is trying to hold us down or hold us back from a blessing the Lord has in store for us. Ephesians 6:12 says, "For we wrestle not against flesh and blood, but against principalities, against powers, against the rulers of the darkness of this world, against spiritual wickedness in high places."

I will speak for myself here, but maybe there are others who can identify with what I am about to say. At times, in my Christian walk, I have found myself in various types of struggles. Sometimes it seems like a battle—a "wrestling match" if you will— for a victory in some aspect of life. There have been financial battles, health battles, and intercessory battles for a friend or a loved one.

Sometimes I feel the battle rages in my heart, but mostly I realize that the battle is in my mind. This is because I know that the Lord has already made provision for us, but for some reason I cannot see it or feel it, or find it in the area of my distress.

Some of my most difficult, prolonged battles occurred when I was seeking the Lord for His will in my life and seeking purpose and fulfillment in my own life, especially as I have entered the season of retirement.

I did not win every time I stepped on the mat, but it did not cause me to quit or give up. Sometimes life deals a crushing blow, but as a child of God, we can take assurance in Romans 8:28 where it says, "and we know that all things work together for good to them that love God, to them that are called according to His purpose." Now, I do not believe for one second that God causes bad things to happen, but I believe that He can take any situation and cause some good to come out of it.

When we find ourselves in a struggle, call upon the name of Jesus to intercede for us. Joy can be a weapon to benefit us. Choose joy, because "The joy of the Lord is our strength." (Nehemiah 8:10). In wrestling, we had particular attire to participate in the sport. This attire was designed to help us as we tried to maneuver and implement our offensive and defensive moves. When needed, we should put on "The garment of praise for the spirit of heaviness." (Isaiah 61:3)

In Psalm 91:1-3, we are told that if we dwell in the secret place of the most high, we shall be under the shadow of the Almighty. He is our refuge and fortress, and He shall deliver us from the "snare of the fowler." That snare—according to Matthew Henry, an esteemed commentator from the seventeenth century — "Is an unseen trap laid for the unwary prey." Psalm18:2, says the Lord is my rock and fortress, and deliverer…

When life or the devil has us down, do not give up—EVER! In my matches, when it was clear that my opponent had me down—the cheerleaders would cheer—"Get up Sam, get up." Actually, this annoyed me a little, because of course I WANTED to get up—what were they thinking? When you are down, you always want to get up, don't you?… DON'T YOU? I hope so.

There was another wrestling term that we used on occasion. It was "going in the tank," which meant that someone was giving up. The Lord never wants us to "go in the tank" or give up.

Listen to the cheerleaders: your friends, pastor, trusted family members—all in our "cloud of witnesses" that want to help and cheer us on when needed. Be inspired by them and their desire to motivate you to victory in the battles of your life. Don't forget to be a cheerleader in someone else's life—the outcome of their struggle might depend on it!

The Day Honey Died

We have all heard the phrase "A dog is man's best friend." Qualities of a good pet include obedience, loyalty, comfort in good times and bad, willingness to put the master above itself, and perhaps as a greeter at the end of a long, trying day. These are qualities we would do well to exemplify in our lives as well.

Honey was a dog my family and I rescued from a local S.P.C.A. when she was just a puppy. My daughters were in middle school at the time, and they named her because of her honey coloring. She was a Retriever/Collie mix with a pinkish red nose when most other dogs had a black nose. She had been abandoned on the S.P.C.A. doorstep in a box with several of her siblings. It wasn't long before we realized how frightened she was of loud noises; thunder, gunshots and fireworks. It seemed excessive, which made us wonder about her early experiences. Was she abused or subjected to unusual conditions? She certainly seemed happy to be in her new home.

When we begin our walk with the Lord, we experience joy, excitement and the love that a new relationship with the Father brings to us. However, we may still carry some fears from our life's journey. In Psalm 37:4, we read that the Lord relieves us of all our fears as we grow and trust in Him.

Honey was a very hyper dog. Every thunderstorm she would try desperately to get into our bedroom, eventually ending up in our bed between me and my wife, and if possible, under the covers. It was nothing for her to tear through a door, and once through a window to try to escape loud noises.

When our kids played with the neighbor friends, our dog would not think twice about ripping the stockade fence apart just to get to be with our girls and play. It was a trying time for me, and I got to the point where I decided to return Honey to the S.P.C.A. I hoped that someone would be able to deal with and help relieve some of her fears. When I asked what would become of her, I was told that if she wasn't adopted within two weeks, she would be put down. I could not bear it, so I told Honey to "Get back in the truck!" We were going home!

There is a line in the movie *Seabiscuit,* which says, "You don't give up on someone just because they are banged up a little." Our Lord never gives up on us just because we are beat up a little——or much! I've heard it said that there is nothing we can do to make God love us more, and nothing we can do —or have done—that will make God love us less.

So a couple of years went by and Honey had not gotten much better. She was a good dog; friendly with the kids, but still so hyper. I thought it noble to place an ad in my church bulletin trying to find Honey a new home. When my Pastor—who was a dog lover himself —saw the ad, he read it aloud from the pulpit. He then asked, "Who is it that would want to give away their dog? That's not right"! I sheepishly raised my hand, apologizing, then rescinding my ad and restoring Honey to her permanent home.

My Pastor, Woodson Moore, was among many other wonderful things, in the restoration business. He never wanted to throw anyone away. There was a time in my life when he should have thrown me away—but he did not. I had not been living true to my Christian testimony. Pastor addressed my shortcomings and the restoration had begun. Had he handled things differently, it is conceivable I might have left the church. He restored my standing instead of discarding me. It is no stretch to say my life, as well as the lives of my children, could have been altered drastically.

In Jeremiah 30:17, the Lord says "But I will restore you to health and heal your wounds, declares the Lord." (NIV) Our "health" can be physical, emotional, societal, and more. The wounds could be a variety of things as well, including circumstances from poor choices in life or hurts from friends and loved ones. The Lord sees us and wants to restore us, just where we are.

So Honey was part of our family for fourteen years. The inevitable always comes. Common to larger dogs, her back legs began to give out. I had to carry her up and down the steps each day to get her outside. Her one hundred and ten pounds were difficult for me to manage at times. Her spirit was still good, but the time came when we had to come to a decision to say goodbye, for her benefit. It was a difficult day for my wife and me.

We could not bring ourselves to do so the week before Christmas, so a few days after New Year's we finally called the Vet. We wanted to make Honey's final resting place at our home. My heart was heavy knowing what lay ahead. I carried Honey to our SUV. The Vet came outside to our car and put Honey to her final rest as I held her in my arms. My wife and I cried like babies. Anyone who has had a similar experience will understand. Will I see Honey again someday? I believe so. The Bible speaks of animals in heaven, so why not? I remember watching a movie with my kids when they were young – *All Dogs go to Heaven*. So there you go!

Of course a pet is not a person, but somehow they find a way to become part of our family. Honey was a wonderful pet for so many years. I am glad I did not mess that up. We all grieve terribly at the loss of a friend and a loved one. When we know the individual was a follower of Jesus, though the loss still hurts, we can have that "Blessed Hope." We will be reunited with them in Heaven. Imagine how our Heavenly Father feels when individuals choose not to follow Him and partake of His eternal fellowship. We can be an example and witness —to be salt and light to our loved ones and to the world to help them find their way to eternity.

Let's be about our Father's business

A Theory For Everything

The 2014 movie *The Theory of Everything,* depicted the life of Stephen Hawking, the British astrophysicist. No one can call into question the brilliance of Mr. Hawking who passed away in 2018. Despite his physical disabilities, his mind functioned at a level foreign to most of humankind. Many of us may have the tendency, or at least temptation, to accept things such a brilliant person might say as truth or proven fact. No disrespect is intended in these words.

In his lifetime Hawking did much to advance our knowledge of science as he applied known laws and tested theories that might become new laws or remain yet unproven. I can only imagine the drive and excitement that propels one to study in such a field as his. Many ideas still remain theories. Perhaps it is not for man to know all things while we are alive on this earth. I believe that we are born with a desire to learn, to know, and to understand. I believe that science was made for mankind in order to explore and learn, and hopefully reveal the laws governing creation that were set in motion by the Creator. In reality, it is not important to know everything now. I am reminded of the verse in Proverbs 25:2, where it says "It is the glory of God to conceal a thing; but the honor of kings to search out a matter."

A quote that explains Mr. Hawking's theory about life after death is as follows: "I regard the brain as a computer which will stop working when its components fail. There is no heaven or after life for broken down computers. That is a fairy story for people afraid of the dark." (*Time Magazine*).

Now since Hawking did not possess "all knowledge," this must have been a theory—or a hope —a dangerous one on which to risk one's existence in eternity. The Bible clearly contradicts his beliefs. It says there is a heaven and a hell, and eternity exists in both places. Now of course, this assumes that one believes in the Bible at all. Whether we make a conscious decision or not, we all put our trust in some belief— in this case, the Bible, God's Word, or a statement or belief similar to Mr. Hawkings'.

If I am a believer of the Bible and its promise of life after death, and if I am wrong and Mr. Hawking is right, then when I die my life passes into nothingness. The only thing that I have lost would have been my beliefs. Time for me will be no more.

On the other hand, if what the Bible says is true about life after death— and where we will spend it—and I do not believe what the Bible says—then I will have lost everything for eternity. Essentially, I will have traded peace, joy, companionship, and light, for torment, sadness, loneliness, and eternal darkness. In the 1989 movie, *Indiana Jones and the Last Crusade*, the brave knight guarding the cup of Christ tells Indiana that he must "Choose wisely." We should all heed his advice!

Mr. Hawking once said, "My goal is simple. It is the complete understanding of the universe, why it is as it is, and why it exists at all." I remember teaching a sixth grade Sunday School class over forty years ago and asking the kids, "Why would God make so much in the universe?" A young lady looked up at me and simply said, "For His glory." I said, "Okay then." Psalm 19:1 says, "The heavens declare the glory of God; and the firmament showeth his handiwork."

Theories are not proven fact. The "Big Bang Theory" suggests one massive explosion containing all of the matter necessary to create what we know in the universe. As matter expanded, all of the stars, planets, galaxies and other known entities simply came into existence. In Genesis, God explains how and in what order things were created. In Job 38: 1-7, God asks Job where he was when God laid the foundations of the world.

Evolution is taught as if it were proven fact, when it is only a theory held together by very questionable reasoning. Contrast that with the account of creation, and the miracle of life—in particular, reproduction and the procreation of every species designed by God. Psalm 100:3 says, "Know ye that the Lord he is God: it is he that made us." Psalm 139: 14 says, "I am fearfully and wonderfully made."

Let's not forget the "Titanic theory." Some builders and passengers of the Titanic said "Not even God himself could sink that ship." Obviously that was not fact, just a theory, or hope from those who thought they were certain about the matter.

It is all about where we derive our basis of truth, our faith, if you will. One might say that it takes a lot of faith to believe there is a God, and that He simply created everything as we see it in the universe, and that the miracle of life was His design for the human race. I believe it takes less faith to believe that God Almighty set these things in motion, than it does to believe that all of the stars and planets just happened to line up in galaxies. Then by coincidence, the earth has just the right composition to sustain our life.

In addition, we, as creation, just came about by millions of years of trial and error until all of the perfect components of life were aligned in the pool of primordial ooze, eventually resulting in all of the various life forms among us? I liken this to any scrap yard that contains components necessary to assemble a running car. Given enough time the components will align themselves and will eventually come together and assemble a vehicle that on its own will drive out of the yard.

In a recent post by Rev. Franklin Graham, he tells the story of eleven year old William Maillis, a college graduate, who wants to be an astrophysicist and have his doctorate by age eighteen. When asked why he wanted to be an astrophysicist, young William replied, "I want to prove to the world that God does exist through science." Go for it kid!

The Bible says there is everlasting life in heaven for those who believe on the Lord Jesus Christ (John 3:16). Also, He is preparing many mansions (John 14:2). It describes the brilliant light and the New Jerusalem,

(Revelation 21:2) a place of praise and worship and joy. (Revelation 19:1) "Eye hath not seen, nor ear heard, neither have entered into the heart of man, the things God hath prepared for them that love him." (1 Corinthians 2:9)

The alternative is described as a dark, bottomless pit. God is not there, and there will be no companionship. In the book, *Dante's Inferno*, Dante describes the sign at the Gate of Hell. It reads, "Abandon hope, all ye who enter here." Try to imagine a place without any hope—a feeling likely experienced by the builders of the Titanic as the ship was about to sink to the bottom of the ocean.

I hope Mr. Hawking had the Truth revealed to him. We will all come face to face with the Truth at some point. Psalm 14:1 says, "The fool has said in his heart that there is no God." We are not forced to believe one way or the other. We get to choose, so "Choose wisely."

Don't Play In The Garbage Can

Exactly how far **IS** the east from the west? In Psalm 103:12 we are told that our transgressions are cast as far as the east is from the west. Sounds far, doesn't it? But how far? Imagine yourself standing on a large, vast plain and you are facing east. Behind you then would be west. When you take a step east, west is still behind you! Repeat this as many times as you like, but west will never catch up to you!

Teaching in past classes, I would give the example of how we could start on one side of the room, be constantly walking toward the other side, yet never reach the opposite side. We start by taking ten steps, then half as many (5), then half as many (2 ½), again half as many (1 ¼) steps. We can repeat this over and over, but we will never reach the opposite side! For the football fan, you would know the expression when a penalty is enforced near the goal line to be "half the distance to the goal"...Question: how many penalties would it take to reach the goal line? Hmm? Right—by taking half the distance each time——you will NEVER reach the goal line! NEVER! In that sense, the goal line is infinitely away! That's far.

All of us have a past. All of us have sinned (Romans 3:23), but the Lord is faithful to forgive those sins and cast them away. Sometimes we have difficulty in forgiving ourselves and possibly forgetting those past sins as the Lord forgets. We are washed white as snow because of the blood of Jesus. Grasp this as it is intended for us.

We are all familiar with the term "garbage can." Each day we place discarded items —used, spoiled, or no longer of use in the can awaiting the proper means of final removal. I believe that we have a "spiritual garbage can" as well, into which we gladly throw our past sins, and as we ask forgiveness, Jesus will empty that can.

We should never play in our garbage cans. Although our sins are forgiven, the memories sometimes lurk there for our lifetime, and revisiting them definitely goes against the doctor's orders. I remember as a kid we would gather the trash cans of family and neighbors and take them to the dump. In one area we even had a neighborhood landfill, where it was fun to hang out. UGH! Although an adventure as kids, danger lurked there in many forms. We should not have been playing around garbage.

The spiritual garbage can could also be a dwelling place (home) to other hazardous entities. The what ifs, past hurts, feelings of jealousy, or even hate may reside in our garbage can.

The garbage of what ifs could cause us to lose focus on God's blessings for us today. We could be wasting time and energy on matters from our past where we have no control at this point in our lives. If only I had gone to the other college, chosen the other occupation, or married the other person. If only I had been there, at that time, things would have been different.

Personally, I have a "what if" which still lingers. As a result of my work schedule many years ago, I missed an opportunity to help someone who was very dear to me and in need. Had I been in my normal place on that particular day, the life of this individual would be drastically different. I need to understand the result of my not being in my usual place is in no way my fault, but to this day I have difficulty in letting go of the thoughts. I could have changed the course of her life. To dwell in this part of the garbage can will only be detrimental. When we are looking back, it is always difficult to look forward.

Past hurts, jealousy, unforgiveness, and feelings of hate certainly are garbage items we need to properly dispose. We cannot leave these things hanging around in our lives. The Bible is clear that we need to be forgiving. There will be times when we extend forgiveness and it will be accepted. Other times it may not be accepted. Nevertheless, we will have done what is required of us. A good friend once said in one of our Bible study groups, "Yes, we are called to forgive, but it does not mean that the relationship is always restored." Past hurts sometimes take long to decompose. Their shelf life is long.

Jealousy can be debilitating if we allow it to rule our thoughts and actions. In a relationship, it could actually drive away the person we love. Jealousy can also keep us from being happy when a friend receives a blessing or honor, instead filling us with resentment garbage.

If we leave hate in the garbage can without dealing with the issues, we are setting ourselves up for self inflicted wounds. In Proverbs 10:12 we are told "Hatred stirs up conflict, but love covers all wrongs." (NIV) I read recently an account where former Senator Alan Simpson was quoted as saying at the funeral of President George H.W. Bush, that "Hatred corrodes the container that carries it." Hatred will corrode our hearts and lives if we harbor this garbage can dweller.

The initial idea for this article came about because of a discussion I had with one of my spiritual mentors. We were about to discuss a topic from the past and suddenly she said, "No, I don't want to play in the garbage can." It was not a bad or hurtful topic, just something that really did not need to be revisited. It has been years since that discussion until this writing. Why do I write this now? I don't know. Maybe you can answer that for yourselves.

Finally, knowing we all have garbage cans, remember to properly dispose of unwanted, harmful items. They can become smelly, rotten aspects and influences. However, if we peek into it but don't play inside, we can learn valuable lessons from our past. We can experience healing, learn forgiving, and be wary of items to avoid. We can learn from our mistakes in the past for ourselves, perhaps to the benefit of others as well.

The Brain Tumor

We were running late for church one Sunday in early March of 2019. As I closed the house door behind me and started down the steps toward the car, my wife was waiting patiently for me. I received a text message. I really did not have time to read it at that moment, but it was from a former student; one with whom I had not had a conversation in nearly ten years. I decided to read it once in the car, as I could not imagine what she might be writing about.

The text read as follows: Hi Mr. Siligato, this is Mickie. I don't always tell people when I pray for them, but last night in the middle of the night I was awakened by the Lord. My eyes were not opened yet and I saw an image of you and heard the Lord say, "Pray for Sam Siligato," so I did, and still am. The Lord also said to tell you, "I hear you, I see you, and I have prayer warriors lifting you up."

Now in a way it was uplifting and encouraging to know the Lord told her to pray for me. The Lord knows our names and can impress upon us to be sensitive in our spirits to pray for others in a time of need. In Genesis sixteen, we find the story of Hagar. She calls the Lord El Roi, meaning "you are the God who sees me," and in Psalm 20:1, we are told that the Lord hears us in our time of trouble and distress. Interesting that Hagar's son Ishmael's name means God hears us.

I distinctly remember my initial reaction upon reading the text. The thought, then concern, that something may be wrong with me. I had been having headaches and neck aches for months. I attributed that to a combination of work and my older age. One of my jobs was painting. I was sixty four at the time. We all get aches and pains from time to time, but this time the pains had persisted. I had just returned from a missions trip to Florida doing some hurricane relief work, and at the time I was hoping the warmer weather would help me physically. I was becoming increasingly concerned but still resisted calling the doctor.

Finally at the urging of my wife and daughters, I reluctantly made a doctor appointment. I am blessed by a loving, caring, God fearing wife of thirty seven years. Proverbs 31:30 tells me "that a woman who fears the Lord is to be praised." My three grown and married daughters have always been "arrows in my quiver," to pray for and encourage Dad.

On March 7, 2019, my wife was away on a women's retreat. I had to serve communion in our church service that day. My sister sat with me, and as we were sitting there a congregant who was directly behind us stood up and gave a word to the church. He said, "We are healed by His blood and His stripes, have NO fear!" Then he sat down. I remember thinking to myself, "Lord, is that for me?" Just then my sister leaned over and said, "Brother, that was for you!"

I usually read two or three daily devotionals, and when a particular one speaks out to me, I will mark it and eventually tear it out for future reference. On March 17, 2019, one week after the text was received, I read a very familiar verse which was the main thrust of the devotion. Joshua 1:9 says, "Be strong and of good courage; BE NOT AFRAID, NEITHER BE THOU DISMAYED; For the Lord thy God is with thee withersoever thou goest." I have read this verse numerous times, but this devotion continued…"Do not be afraid or terrified for whatever darkness looms for you." I wondered, is something going to happen to me?

The next devotion I cut out was on April 12, 2019. It began, "Sometimes when people receive life threatening news they encounter a paralyzing fear." Oh yes, that was becoming me as I was wondering what in the world was going on. In 2 Timothy 1:7, we are told that the Lord does not give us the spirit of fear, but of power, and of love, and of a sound mind. The article continued mentioning that the writer was facing brain surgery.

A CAT scan was scheduled for Friday, April 12 at eleven a.m. I did errands earlier in the day and told my wife we could pack a lunch and take it to a nearby beach to wind down. By the time I arrived at home from my appointment, my doctor had already called and told my wife I needed to get to the hospital right away for an MRI because the CAT scan showed a mass in my brain. I would have rather gone to the picnic lunch. Lunch ruined! Anxiety was of course building.

My wife and I went to the local ER. I asked my wife to call our friends who were hosts of our Bible study group to begin to pray. As I entered the ER, I was expecting the normal hours long wait, especially since there were others ahead of me. However, I was called ahead of the others after a short ten minute wait. I was getting even more concerned.

The MRI confirmed the growth that the CAT scan had found; a tumor in the front of my brain, which the local doctors planned to remove on Monday, two days later. After prayer and consultations, we decided to travel to Jefferson Hospital in Philadelphia for the surgery. The following day I was transported to Jefferson Hospital, and the doctors there planned the surgery for Tuesday, April 16.

While waiting in the hospital that Palm Sunday, April 14, my scripture for the day's devotion was Isaiah 41:10. "Fear thou not; for I am with thee; be not dismayed; for I am thy God: I will strengthen thee; yea will help thee." Good timing Lord! Now believe this or not, the devotion went on to tell the story about a woman who had an inoperable brain tumor! That was not the case with me, but I was not looking forward to my surgery for sure.

When we face uncertainties we must grasp the Lord's peace and grasp the assurance that He is always with us no matter what. Matthew 28:20 says, "And surely I am with you always, to the very end of the age." (NIV) Once again, a timely devotion ministered to my Spirit.

That same day my oldest daughter, who was expecting her second girl, asked questions of the doctors. I was counseled to conflicting opinions as to whether or not the tumor and surrounding area would be cancerous. Even though the news was not the best, I had a peace about me. Honestly, I have not experienced such a peace when I was faced with lesser challenges in my life.

Later that afternoon, my spiritual Mom and sister visited, bringing a card signed by many of my church friends. Their words of encouragement and prayers were strength to me. We should always know that there is life and strength in the words that we share. I was very grateful for them.

In my younger years I loved playing baseball and softball. My position was mostly shortstop. I was good at my position. I could get anything hit to either side or overhead as much as I could leap. My lifelong ball playing friends and I joke that the older we get, the better we were! The ground balls I had the most trouble with were the slow rollers hit straight towards me. Perhaps, I believe, I had too much time to think about those. The hard hit balls did not leave much time to think, only pure reaction in most cases.

My tumor episode happened so fast. There was no time to think and let an overwhelming fear grip me. The Lord had been sending me messages through scripture, devotions, and friends. I made up my mind to trust Him no matter what, and I cannot explain it so much, but I had that peace that "passes all understanding" during that time. (Philippians 4:7)

Surgery was scheduled for first thing on Tuesday, April 16. I received messages from my Pastor and close friends very early that morning. I had family there, and we prayed before I was taken to the operating room. Several hours later the surgery was complete. There was excruciating pain, but that subsided within a day. The biopsy showed that the tumor was benign. Thank you Jesus! Recovery was quick and I did not need post-op treatment or much medication. It has been several years now and there are sensations sometimes because of the titanium plate in my head, and I still have to limit a few of my activities, but all is well!

I am thankful for God's Word, His peace, and for those I have as friends and family who were praying for me. Many churches in many parts of the country were praying as well as they received word about my surgery. (All were my prayer warriors, I believe, as mentioned in the initial text from my former student).

The Lord saw me and heard me even before I knew I needed Him. He knows our comings and goings, even the very number of hairs on our head. He also says He will never leave us or forsake us. That is good to know!

One New Thing

(*The Deal Fell Through*)

I n Isaiah 43: 18-19 we read, "Forget the former things; do not dwell on the past. See, I am doing a new thing! Now it springs up; do you not perceive it"? (NIV) I was at the point of needing a "new thing," and in that particular moment I did not perceive it.

If you are a Realtor, as I am, or the spouse of a Realtor, you have undoubtedly experienced the disappointment and heartbreak of a deal that fell apart—perhaps only a few days from closing. For those who are not a Realtor, maybe I could get you in the moment. The feeling is like being punched in the stomach and having the wind knocked out of you. A sound that might fit is that of a toilet flushing. A Realtor does not get paid until the closing or settlement occurs. If a property fails to close, all of the time and effort invested becomes fruitless; and I was hearing that sound.

Four months prior, after a church service, a good friend and I were talking about a situation in his life. He said Philippians 3:13-14, had ministered to him. I must admit, the verse did not pop into my head immediately, but I made a note and was determined to research the scripture. I wrote the scripture on my clipboard that I used daily for my business and personal to do list each week. Of course I intended on researching the scripture as soon as possible. However, it did not happen. I would transfer that scripture, without knowing what it said, from week to week on my clipboard —for four months! I know, strange.

Fortunately, there were not many transactions that failed to close in my thirty plus years experience. This story comes from one that did fail to close —an investment property that was my own, one on which I labored countless hours for over seven months infusing much capital. The finished product was a very desirable, spacious house, having been resurrected from a terrible eyesore—a total renovation of all components. I was finally ready to sell.

I truly felt the pain for my clients when it was their property that did not close. Emotional and financial hurts can be devastating. Add logistical problems like moving, trying to settle on a new property at the same time, lining up utilities and taking off work. It just gets very complicated. Many people are affected.

Within a week of listing the house for sale, we had a contract. This process usually takes about forty five days to complete the closing. Things can happen, and they do—which can cause delays, bumps in the road, and sometimes more serious problems that could jeopardize a sale.

Sometimes life can be like that too. Cruising along, we might encounter bumps that slow us down. Maybe a pothole will knock us out of alignment temporarily. Unexpected events or tragedies might threaten to knock us out, or at least derail us from our calling or purpose in life.

As time passed, the transaction encountered problems on the buyer's end, especially with the mortgage. In real estate as in other fields, one can see problems as "flags flying." Yellow caution flags, and red ones signal that the deal is in real trouble. So the flags flew, and the deal finally tanked one week before closing.

Spiritual "flags," I believe from the Holy Spirit, can serve as caution and warnings to keep us from doing something that might not be in our best interest. We should heed the nudging from God's spirit—be alert to what He might be trying to tell us and prepare a plan to avoid the potholes and damaging decisions in life.

I was devastated. As I moped around the house, I sat on my porch just feeling sorry for myself—— not my most stellar Christian moment.

My wife joined me—surely for consolation and support——-I thought. She looked at me, pointed her finger and said, "I give you until tomorrow morning to get out of that mood!" What? I could not believe she said that! Now I will speak for myself here, because I doubt this applies to any of you, but there have been times in my life when I just wanted to have a pity party. The Bible says to "put on the garment of praise for the spirit of heaviness." I did not reach for that garment at that particular time.

Instead, I went to my desk and grabbed my clipboard just to see about things I needed to do. I noticed the scripture I had jotted down —as I said—four months prior. I took the opportunity to finally look up the verse. Philippians 3:13-14 says, "But one thing I do; forgetting what is behind and straining forward to what is ahead. I press on toward the goal to win the prize for which God has called me heavenward in Christ Jesus."(NIV) I took the verse personally. I needed this now.

The verses hit me like a ton of bricks. Isn't God's timing perfect? I felt the Lord telling me to forget what just happened and look forward. Also, the important goal was not the sale of the house, but the "prize" that calls me heavenward. Do struggles in life sometimes cause us to take our eyes off the prize, if only temporarily? Though the sale fell through, I still felt a great accomplishment in the renovation, and I had faith that the house would eventually sell.

As I continued to pray on the porch, I felt God say that all would be well with my property. Also, that there would be five additional new sales in a very short time. At that time the real estate market was stable but not terrific in my area. Five sales anytime, especially then, was not a likely scenario. Before retiring I thanked the Lord for His Words and comfort. I had been reminded that I should give thanks in all things.

The next morning, during my morning devotion, the phone rang. It was another agent from the same office which had submitted the original offer on my house. The first agent had explained how the deal ended, and would you believe that the second agent had a buyer who just lost out on another house and was in the market for a home just like my property? Not only that, but this new buyer was working with a very reputable mortgage company—the same one I used for most of my business. Imagine that!

The new buyer loved the house. We went under contract for the same price, and the deal was on its way. Before I finish the story with these new buyers, I need to say that within one week, four new deals came my way. I believe this was the Lord honoring the impression I received that morning on the porch. The Lord is faithful! Sometimes our answers come immediately, but often they do not. We need to stand as our faith is tested.

The new buyers were a very nice family who could certainly use the five bedrooms and multiple baths. They were Christians who had lost the previous home through the fault of the seller. The wife explained to me, they had prayed for a miracle, and my house could be a blessing to them, and that she and her husband considered it a miracle how things worked out for them. She did not know that I had been praying for a similar miracle. Romans 8:28 came to mind, in that it says that all things work for good to those who love the Lord. God can find a way to bring good from a difficult situation or heartache.

I was so happy for them! I just wanted to give her a hug, but thought it might not be appropriate. On the day of the inspections, a good portion of the family was present including parents, grandparents, and a few cousins. As we all stood in the front yard she again told her story of disappointment with the first house, and the joy of God's blessing to find my house with the interesting circumstances. She began to cry as she related the story—then looked at me and asked—can I give you a hug? I got all choked up and said, "Absolutely!"

Revisiting Isaiah 43:19, "Behold I do a new thing." He certainly did for both of our families! The verse continues to say that the Lord is making a way in the wilderness and streams in the wasteland. Could these streams be blessings in times of struggle and sorrow when we might feel like we are in a wilderness wasteland? Employment loss, divorce, financial challenges, death of a loved one, or health challenges——any of which could make us feel like we are in a wilderness.

What "wasteland" experiences have you encountered only to have the Lord provide a stream of encouragement, blessings, or new life? You might remember the following catchy tune from a long time past…

Count your blessings name them one by one,
Count your many blessings see what God hath done!

They Had No Means

It is always wise to try and live within our means. Incurring unnecessary debt can be crippling and hold us in financial bondage. We are commanded to be good stewards—not because the Lord wants to deny us good things in life, but because He wants to see us flourish. Having a particular amount of money in the bank should not be the defining benchmark for our success or happiness. Joy and happiness can be products of many other things in life.

On a recent missions trip to the Florida panhandle, I joined a group of friends from my church to do some hurricane relief work in the aftermath of hurricane Michael. When we arrived, the devastation we witnessed was immense—in some places unimaginable. The trees; thousands of them, all laid horizontal in the same direction. Roof tops by the hundreds were damaged or missing altogether. Debris was strewn about, and so much was heaped in piles either from the storm itself or the beginning work of the massive cleanup effort.

We were housed in a service building of a local church. We attended a church service the first morning. I remember being surprised by the attitude of the people who attended, because they seemed happy and joyful. Considering what the community had just endured, I would have expected the atmosphere to be more somber.

We read in Philippians chapter four, that Paul says he was content in whatever state he was in. That can be a challenge at times. The congregants exhibited "the joy of the Lord", and it was apparent that "joy" was the source of their strength. They welcomed us and were so appreciative because we had sacrificed our time and money to travel and be a help to them.

Some of the members we got to know a little more closely during our visit. Our social time was limited as there was much work to be done. John was the coordinator that would line up the work we would be doing throughout the week. The work consisted of anything a family needed, including moving debris, downed trees, and roof needs. We spent a couple of days organizing supplies and removing trees and branches from the church property. We went there to serve and bless, but as is always the case when I went on such trips, I was the one being blessed. Consider this for a moment maybe when we have an opportunity to do a favor or be a blessing to someone—it is really WE who are being given the favor of a blessing.

So each day we were given a list of addresses to visit and work and minister. Sometimes we knew ahead what work we would be doing, other times we found out only when we arrived. We were not made aware of the financial status of families we would be helping, but the impression I had after visiting each home was that these people were hurting and had suffered losses that would be difficult to overcome.

Early in the week at our first stop, our group worked tirelessly removing debris from an older couple's yard. I remember wondering how this could possibly help, but afterward realized, if nothing else—perhaps the organized yard would at least bring a sense of peace from the chaos the yard represented just a short time earlier. Before we left, we were asked if we would go inside and pray for the wife who had been bed ridden. One in our group, Wayne, prayed, and the woman appeared to be responsive. The husband told us that it was the first time she had responded in several days. We were all touched in that moment.

One stop was a manufactured home near a river on the outskirts of town. We needed to do roof work, porch repair, interior work, and needed to help move furniture throughout the home. The elderly single woman was so grateful and appreciative. She offered to pay us, but that was not why we were there. We asked if we could pray with her, and she said yes, but needed to tell us of some personal requests that were burdening her. So Dan, another volunteer, led, and we prayed. This was why we were there.

The next day one of the stops was for a couple whose home needed minor repairs which were quickly accomplished. The owners then told us of their neighbor whose home had sustained much damage, especially the roof. The owners did not know if their neighbors were people of faith. So our team went to the neighbors. Our team leader, Steve, assessed the situation and was off to purchase the necessary materials. While he was getting supplies, a few of us knocked on the door of another neighbor to see if they needed any help. The single grandmother needed some things cleaned up in her yard which we were able to do in a short amount of time. When Steve returned with the materials, our entire group began to work on the roof of the neighbor who had not even been on our list. The old house had been severely damaged in the storm. The front porch, where the couple was still living, had a roof that looked as if it would collapse at any time. The house was a disaster. I couldn't imagine anyone living there, but they had nowhere to go.

We completed the work for the day, packed up, and returned to the church building. I felt heaviness in my heart for the couple we just visited. Later that evening, I went to our team leader Steve and told him how I felt that I had missed an opportunity to bless the couple. I realized that the Lord had impressed upon my heart to give them money before we left, and I did not do so. I knew we would not be returning as we had other work to accomplish.

Steve told me that he had felt the same for himself, and yes, normally we would not be returning, but there was something else that he wanted to do there. During dinner, Steve and I shared our thoughts with Dan, who proceeded to tell us that he was feeling exactly the same and that he wanted to give the couple some money, but hadn't. The Lord was giving us all another opportunity. Confirmation is always a good feeling too!

When we returned the next day, after completing the work, our small group took up an offering which totaled about $250.00. Steve presented the offering and asked if we could pray with them. We all formed a circle in their yard, holding hands as we prayed for them. They were so grateful. They were literally down to their last meal, not knowing what they would do for food the next day. The circle broke up and we started to head to the van. Before the couple would say good-bye, they asked if THEY could pray for US! This couple had NOTHING as far as the material world was concerned, but what they offered was EVERYTHING they could offer—prayers of gratitude and for our well being, and for our willingness to come and help them. Once we returned to the church at the end of the day, the project leader John told us that he knew of the couple we just helped. He said, "You know the expression that people live above or below their means? These people HAD NO MEANS!

You've probably heard the terms "take away" and "Ah ha" moments. That day, as I gathered in the circle with my friends and coworkers, watching the couple with NO MEANS pray for us —was my "Ah ha" moment! My "take away" was the blessing that I received from the couple and the Lord. I will never forget that moment.

The widow in Mark chapter 12:41-44, and Luke chapter 21:1-4, who gave her last mites, certainly did not give much as far as man was concerned, but she gave ALL she had. She is remembered to this day! May we all strive to be faithful servants, and be open to the leading of the Holy Spirit so that we may not miss any opportunities to bless others—and to bless ourselves too!

Finish Well

The third quarter of the most important game of the team's season had ended. It had been a back and forth battle to this point with exciting plays and times of struggles. On the sideline the coach raised his hand in the air with fist clenched. He then extended four fingers and turned in each direction among his players and emphatically thrust his hand high in the air. Four. Four. Four! In football that signifies the start of the fourth quarter, but the deeper meaning is "This is it, now or never. Now is the time, give it all you have left and finish the game on a high note." The coach might continue to exhort his players. "I know you are tired, but pick yourself up, you can do this, we have to finish this!" Hebrews 12:12 exhorts in a similar way when it says, "Wherefore lift up the hands which hang down, and the feeble knees."

In many ways life is like a contest— a race perhaps. Paul says in 2 Timothy, that he ran his race and finished his course. There are highs and lows in life, beautiful peaceful days and storms too. We all will have battles to fight and victories to celebrate. Each of us is special and unique. We have been given gifts and talents for a special purpose, and no other can fulfill our purpose. Romans 14:12 tells us we all have to give an account of ourselves to God. In other words how did we run our race. Let us echo the words of Jesus when He said "I have glorified thee on earth: I have finished the work which thou gavest me to do." (John 17:4)

Have you ever given thought to what your fourth quarter would be like? What things would you like to accomplish during the final laps in life? What does victory look like and mean to you? Picture for a moment, nearing our finish line as "cheerleaders," the great cloud of witnesses spoken of in Hebrews 12:1, cheer us on. We set aside every weight as we run with patience finishing our race... Ah, almost there!

The race is not won in a day. In "mortal time" (years), the length of our race is different for each one of us. In "spiritual" time all of our lives are likely to be the same in light of eternity. I once heard a speaker at a funeral talking about the 'dash of life.' Each of our gravestones will show it; the year of birth—year of death. The dash represents our lifetime, our "race time," if you will. So the question remains, what will our dash consist of? What will we do in our dash of life? Abraham Lincoln said, "Whatever you do in life, do it well." In Colossians 3:23 we are told, "And whatsoever ye do, do it heartily, as to the Lord, and not unto men."

All of us have been entered into the race. We do not have to *run* if we choose not to, but are responsible for our actions and in-actions during the length of our respective races. The length of our race is not likely categorized as a sprint, but more like a marathon. Marathons are long, grueling races, many times traversing all types of terrain. Open road, mountains, valleys, shady areas, and sometimes extreme heat which can sap the strength from the runner, are likely encounters. All of which are perhaps similar to the terrain we face as we run our course in life.

We must run our race with resolve to overcome every obstacle; resolve to see us through. James 1: 3-4 says, "Because you know that the testing of your faith produces perseverance. Let the perseverance finish its work so that you may be mature and complete, not lacking anything." (NIV) Could we say that perseverance helps us to finish our race successfully and completely? I think so.

As a painter for many years, I recall some daunting jobs. Almost without exception, on the first day of the job I would ask myself, "How in the world am I ever going to get this entire house painted?" The answer of course is one stroke at a time. Our race is one day—even one step at a time. Many times during a difficult or long job I would hit the proverbial wall. Sometimes it felt like I could go no further, and not finish the work. I remember praying to the Lord to help me to continue and finish. Guess what? He did! Have you ever encountered such a wall in life? Push through. Persevere. Galatians 6:9 tells us, "Let us not become weary in doing good, for at the proper time we will reap a harvest if we do not give up." Let's run and do good, and at the finish line we will reap well if we haven't given up!

Have you ever heard the phrase "stay in your own lane"? Yes, perhaps with a negative connotation when people were telling someone to mind their own business. Let's shed a good light on that phrase. In some races runners must stay in their lane in order to avoid entanglement with other runners and to maximize their speed and time. In our race maybe it is God's purpose to keep us in our lane. He would have us run where He puts us. We are all here at this time for a reason. The Lord has us in the race at this time because He chose us to be running at this time and place. We should stay the course and achieve all He has planned for us.

We don't have to be old to qualify for the fourth quarter. I contend that the fourth quarter is more of a "state of being" than a particular age. We can finish our races with joy. Acts 20:24 says, "But none of these things move me, neither count I my life dear unto myself, so that I might finish my course with joy, and the ministry, which I have received of the Lord Jesus, to testify the gospel of the grace of God."

In Genesis chapter five, we read of a man named Enoch. We don't know a great deal about him except he lived 365 years, and had sons and daughters, including Methuselah. Enoch did have one interesting and unusual thing happen to him. He did not die a natural death. It says in verse twenty-four that "God took him." Not to be lost in that supernatural event is the revelation about Enoch, "He was faithful!" In Genesis, it says that "Enoch walked faithfully with God; then he was no more, because God took him away." As we finish our race, let's finish faithfully!

Maybe we have not always run our race faithfully. I am reminded of the parable with the two sons in Matthew 21:28-31, where each son was asked to work in the vineyard. The first son said "I won't work," but he later repented and decided to work after all. The second son said "I will work," but he never showed up to work. Which was the son who finished well? Does God require us to do great things for Him? I think He asks us to be faithful to our lane—our calling, and if we are, then He can do GREAT things through us!

Finally as we are faithful to run our race, we will finish well and leave a legacy. Let it be said of each one of us that we fought the good fight, finished the race, and kept the faith. (2 Timothy 4:7) We can leave a legacy of kindness, hospitality, and worship to name a few.

Another consideration as we are finishing our course is that our legacy doesn't end when our race is over. The baton will be passed to a family or a ministry to be carried in its own race. A life you influenced, a song composed, or a book written during your race, will continue to be an influence in the lives of many after you cross your finish line. A wall plaque which I have owned for decades says, "The greatest use of life is to spend it on something that will outlast it." That something will be our life in eternity and the legacy we leave behind to be an encouragement to others as they run their own race.

Run Well! Finish Well!

Afterword

———⊷∘❦∘⊶———

Salvation is a free gift from God. With it we can be sure of our eternity. If you would like to have this gift and ask the Lord to come into your heart, please pray the following:

"Thank you Jesus, for my life and for coming to die on the cross for my sins. I ask you to forgive my sins and to come into my heart to be my Savior. Your Word says in John 3:16 that whoever believes on you will not perish but have everlasting life. I want everlasting life in your presence. Help me to know the truth about your love for me."

John 8:32 says, "You shall know the truth, and the truth shall make you free."

John 14:6 says "I am the way, the truth, and the life: no man comes to the Father, but by me."

If you said the prayer above, today is your spiritual birthday! I encourage you to obtain a Bible and begin reading God's Word. Find a Bible believing church—-"the good soil"—-in which to "be planted," as you begin your walk with the Lord.

Feedback Page

I would love to hear from you!

Please let me know where you are from, I like to know where the "arrows" have landed.

Did you have a favorite article or identify with a particular story? Were you able to share the book with anyone who was blessed by it?

Please leave a review for us

All comments are appreciated on Amazon, Barnes & Noble, Apple iBooks, or other social media platforms and the email below

Issuesoftheheart55@gmail.com

For bulk purchasing of this book, please contact us at the above email

CPSIA information can be obtained
at www.ICGtesting.com
Printed in the USA
LVHW080736270123
737935LV00008B/609